Fact and Faith

David L. Bartlett

JUDSON PRESS, VALLEY FORGE

FACT AND FAITH

Library of Congress Cataloging in Publication Data

Bartlett, David Lyon, 1941-
    Fact and faith.

    Bibliography: p.
      1. Miracles. 2. Jesus Christ—Resurrection.
I. Title.
BS2545.M5B37   226'.7'066   74-22517
ISBN 0-8170-0654-0

Printed in the U.S.A.

For my parents, whose love was my first miracle.

Acknowledgments

My first debt of thanks is due to the congregation of University Baptist Church, Minneapolis, who not only allow but encourage me to study, teach, and write.

Much of the material in this book grew out of courses taught at the Graduate Theological Union in Berkeley, at United Theological Seminary of the Twin Cities, and at the American Baptist Assembly, Green Lake, Wisconsin. I am grateful to all those students whose questions and suggestions are reflected in the pages which follow.

The section on resurrection is but one more round in an ongoing discussion with George Stroup, now of Princeton Seminary.

Marvel Kingsley typed the manuscript with her usual skill and put up with my foibles with her usual grace.

James B. Nelson and H. Richard Jewell read portions of the manuscript and made helpful comments. My colleague, Dennis Stull, read the entire manuscript and has greatly enriched the book with his suggestions and my life with his friendship.

Minneapolis, August, 1974

Contents

Introduction

When we read the Four Gospels, we discover that they are full of miracle stories and that they reach their climax in the story of one especially spectacular miracle, the resurrection of Jesus of Nazareth from the dead. Nor is the concern with miracles limited to the Four Gospels. The Old Testament tells a number of stories of miracles—Moses leading the people of Israel through the Reed Sea, Elijah raising the widow's son from the dead. The book of Acts attributes miracles to the apostles, and while Paul seems not to stress miracles (though see 2 Corinthians 12:12, where he claims to have worked miracles), at least the one miracle of the resurrection of Jesus is absolutely central to his theology (see 1 Corinthians 15).

These stories of miracles are a problem for us; they seem strangely old-fashioned and alien to the world as we know it. For the most part we do not claim to have seen seas parted or blind men made to see, and certainly we cannot say that we ever saw anyone who was dead miraculously come to life again.

So we are stuck with the problem of interpretation. We cannot simply read the miracle stories and say, "Ah, yes, we know exactly how that is," because we *don't* know exactly how that is, any more than those who told the miracle stories knew about X rays, psychosomatic diseases, or hypnosis. Whether we like it or not, we have to do some kind of explaining.

One explanation is that while we do not see the kind of miracle that is narrated in the New Testament very often these days, those miracles used to happen, and indeed they happened in exactly the way that they are recorded in the Bible. Jesus put his hands on a blind man's eyes, and the blind man could see; Peter told a lame man to get up and walk, and the lame man got up and walked. Most important, Jesus died on the cross, was buried in a tomb for two days, and on the third day he got up—flesh, blood, and bones—left the tomb, and appeared to various of his followers.

Those who think that the miracles of the Bible happened literally as they are recorded often hold that the miracles provide proofs of the validity of the Christian faith. We know that there is a God because when Moses stretched out his rod, the sea parted and the children of Israel went through. We know that Peter and Paul were true apostles because they were able to heal people. We know that Jesus was the Son of God because he cast out demons, helped the lame to walk, withered the fig tree, and gave sight to the blind. Most important and most clearly, we know that Jesus was the Son of God because, after men had put him to death, God raised him to life. The empty tomb and the appearance of Jesus to his followers proves once and for all that he was God's Son.

Another explanation of the miracle stories is much more skeptical about the historical validity of the biblical narratives. Some Christians would say that we do not really know what happened and that indeed it may be that none of the miracles happened as they were narrated. (It may be that "miracles" do not really *happen* at all.) What counts, these people would say, is not the actual event, but the meaning of the event. Whether the miracles happened or not, the miracle stories can give us valuable insights into ourselves and God.

This second explanation takes several forms. Sometimes the miracles are seen as signs, as pointers to the biblical faith that God acts in history. It is not that any particular miracle story points toward a particular act of God; it is rather that all of them symbolize the great affirmation of the Christian faith, that God is at work in human history, that ours is a God who acts.

Sometimes the miracles are seen as illustrations of the unique power of Jesus' personality. Whatever really happened, certainly he had an immense effect on those who met him, and certainly he showed a remarkable compassion for those in need. Jesus' compassion for the leper, for instance, is a sign of God's compassion for his needy children. That is seen to be the point of the miracle stories, whether Jesus actually ever miraculously healed anyone or not.

Sometimes the miracle stories are said to provide moral examples for Christians. The story of the oppressed people of Israel escaping through the sea reminds Christians that we should oppose oppression wherever we find it. The story of the feeding of the five thousand is a reminder that we need to be sensitive to the problem of poverty and to find ways to join in combating hunger among our fellow humans. The healing stories provide an incentive for us to give time and money to medical research, or at the very least to be sympathetic to the sensitivities of the sick and to look out for blind people crossing the street.

Sometimes the miracle stories are said to provide clues to living a life which is full and rich and significant. They are not important in themselves, but only insofar as they help us understand what life is really about. Certainly even in the New Testament there is evidence that miracle stories were sometimes interpreted in this way. In the sixth chapter of John, the miracle of the feeding is not nearly as important as the whole discourse about Jesus as the bread of life and the necessity of following him to discover for ourselves what life is really about. According to this interpretation, even the great miracle of resurrection is not important in itself; it may or may not have "happened." What is important is that the resurrection provides a great symbol of what can happen in our lives; we can "die" to our old, dull, confused, stodgy, self-centered, ugly selves and "rise" to a new, richer, fuller, more loving life. (And certainly any interpretation of resurrection will have to admit that in part Jesus' resurrection *does* provide such a symbol.)

Sometimes the miracle stories are said to provide the occasion for awakening faith. Whether or not the miracles actually happened the way they are supposed to have happened, the miracle story itself can awaken faith in the listener. When we hear the story of Jesus healing the blind man, we say not, "So that's how he came to see," but "Aha! Now *I* see who Jesus is and what he means and what it means to have faith in him." And at the very best, when we hear one of the miracle stories, we can say, "Aha! Now I *do* have faith in Jesus."

Now the trouble with both kinds of explanations is that both leave out something which is very important.

One explanation seems to say: "It is not the present significance of the miracles which matters. What matters is that they *did* happen, and that confirms my faith." And the other explanation seems to say: "It doesn't matter whether the miracles happened, just so the miracle stories mean something to me." Both of these explanations seem inadequate to the complexity and the richness of the biblical faith.

The belief that everything happened literally as it is recorded and that it all proves the validity of the Christian faith ignores the clear indications in the Bible itself that what happened could never be separated from its ongoing meaning. The miracle stories *are* told, not just to prove something, but to tell us who Jesus was and who God is; they are used in part to provide a moral example, to show us what life is really like, and certainly to call us to faith. We shall look, in the pages ahead, at the ways in which the New Testament writers are always forcing us to look beyond the *fact* of the miracle to *faith* in what the miracle means.

And of course there is no way that the miracles can prove the validity of the Christian faith. If the Sea of Reeds (or the Red Sea) parted when Moses stretched out his rod, that proves only that Moses had magical powers, not necessarily that there is a God, and much less that the God is wise and loving and deeply concerned for the welfare of his children. If Jesus made the blind see, that proves only that he knew some powerful magic or medicine, not that he was the Son of God, much less that through him our sins are forgiven and our lives eternally made whole. Even if the tomb was empty and the disciples saw Jesus walking around and shared meals with him, that does not prove that *God* raised Jesus from the dead, much less that in the resurrection God in Christ won the ultimate victory over the forces of sin and death and established the promise of his enduring kingdom.

Faith can take all the miracle stories, even the resurrection, and see in them the clues to God's pervasive presence in the drama of human history; but they do not *prove* anything, or at least they do not prove anything absolutely essential to Christian faith.

On the other hand, it does not make much sense to say that it is the *meaning* of the miracles which counts, whether the miracles ever happened or not.

It does not make much sense to say that the miracles show us that God acts powerfully in human history if, finally, we cannot point to any event and say, "Look; that's one place where God was acting." There is no way that we can have a God who is active in the abstract; he must show up concretely in human history.

It does not make much sense to say that the miracles show us Jesus' concern for healing unless he actually did some healing. It does not make much sense to say that the miracles provide an example of the need for human compassion unless we can at least say that sometime along the way Jesus *did* something which was compassionate.

It does not make much sense to say that Jesus' miracles provide the clue to the fullness of what life is about unless we can take some of them as indications of what *his* life was about. Authentic existence is not very useful to us unless we can point to the places where it existed, unless we can point to the person who authentically did some of those things which can make life rich and full.

It does not make sense to say that the resurrection is the symbol of the way in which God can bring life out of death unless somehow, at least in that one man, Jesus of Nazareth, God did in fact bring life out of death—did turn all our usual expectations upside down and snatched astonishing victory from the very jaws of defeat.

For the Christian faith is faith, of course, but it is not blind faith. Faith does not mean simply dreaming up a subjective view of God which seems best to fit our needs, or making a cosmic bet on the basis of someone's (or some church's) best guess on the way the world hangs together, or answering an abstract word uttered out of the void: "Believe! Believe!"

The Christian faith is the response to God's great enticement. There is no proof, of course; there could be no proof of the immensity of what we believe. But there is no vacuum, either, over against which the faithful must believe in absurdity for the sake of absurdity. There are hints and clues, signs and modest seductions by which God woos us to love him. It may be that to the objective observer a wink looks like a cinder in the eye and a dropped handkerchief is the unfortunate result of slippery fingers. But a lover knows a lure. The events which the New Testament records, including the miracles, are the hints and clues by which the faithful recognize the Lover's invitation. They do not guarantee adoration, but they invite it. Only we need eyes which can recognize a hint when we see it.

God's great enticement, of course, is Jesus Christ, and it is in him that the peculiar mixture of fact and faith finds its focus. He is both Jesus of Nazareth and Jesus the Christ: a real, historical, empirical man, limited and defined by his history like all of us, and the great revealer of who God is and what he is up to among us.

Because he is Jesus of Nazareth, we have no choice but to try to know him historically and no choice but to recognize the limits of what we know. The earliest of the Four Gospels, Mark, was probably written three or four decades after the crucifixion, after the stories about Jesus had been passed on for some years, largely by word of mouth. As far as the miracle stories are concerned, Matthew and Luke largely based their accounts on what they had already found in Mark, which leaves only John as another "independent" source.

Of course none of the Four Gospels pretends to be "objective," "scientific" history. All historical writing has its biases, but here the biases are overwhelmingly evident. The Gospels are not a careful attempt to sort out the facts and present them in systematic fashion; the Gospels are an attempt to plead a case, to persuade the reader to faith, to enlist others in a cause. They are more like propaganda than history.

The great bias which the Gospels all share and which is not shared by historians, as historians, when they write today is that what happened in the life of Jesus of Nazareth was not just a human event, but a divine event—that the actors in the story were actors in a drama whose author and finisher was God himself. There is no way that an historical account can prove an assumption like that, but from beginning to end the Gospel writers worked under that assumption.

When we do the best we can to sort through the biases, to compare the accounts, to decide what may have been added through the years of telling the story, we are sometimes surprised at how little "hard" evidence we have. At best we have the result of a few years' ministry: some memorable sayings; some exorcisms and healings; some disputes; a crucifixion; and then something which is certainly more than history, whatever else it may have been. In some ways when we emerge from the massive literature about Jesus of Nazareth, we are amazed at how little we know.

Furthermore, even given the most complete certainty of the validity of the Gospel accounts, what we do know is not sufficient to prove the validity of the Christian story or to produce the fullness of the believer's faith. We simply cannot move by logical inference, even from the most literal interpretation of the texts, to the richness of the Christian faith. We cannot move by logical inference from even immaculate conception, virgin birth, singing angels, bowing wise men, precocious adolescence, descending dove, remarkable healings, conversations with Moses and Elijah, torn temple curtain, and an empty tomb to God the Creator and Sustainer of the universe incarnate in the man Jesus for our salvation, moving all of human history to its immensely surprising and gracious conclusion. All the history may be true and all the faith valid, but the history does not guarantee the faith. At best it points to it, hints at it, illumines it, enables it; it does not prove or guarantee it. When we have said everything historical we can say about Jesus of Nazareth, we are still not enabled to say: Jesus the Christ. That takes imagination or faith or a love which amazes even the lover.

And yet, there is no Christian faith apart from the tawdry empiricism of a real history, the history of Jesus of Nazareth. The Christian faith is not faith in what God is in himself, but faith in what God is for us; it is faith in God who enters into relationship. Entering into relationship requires activity, and activity produces history. Eternal truths and metaphysical systems may be able to make do with abstract verities. Christian faith is stuck with history. From beginning to end Christian faith is both burdened and illumined with event: creation, exodus, exile, return, birth, teaching, healing, crucifixion, resurrection. None of these events is simply historical, but none of them is separated from history, either, any more than God can be divorced from involvement with history or promoted to a pure principle.

More than that, incarnation itself is surely God's gracious recognition of our incurable empiricism. Not only from the side of our limitations, but also from the side of his mercy, God becomes known in events. Jesus Christ represents God's acknowledgment that for us mere people to know grace we must be able to stare it in the face, and to know love we must hold and be held by real and tangible flesh. Such flesh the Word became: entering into events as concrete and oddly historical as birth and death, miracles and resurrection.

Therefore this study will focus on the miracles of Jesus of Nazareth and on the resurrection of Jesus of Nazareth, on the events which were part of a central Event, in the hope that we may come to a clearer understanding and a braver affirmation of a Christianity which can embrace both fact and faith.

CHAPTER 1

Interpreting the Miracles

In the Bible, at least, a miracle is not just an odd event, not even an extraordinarily odd event. People who have no belief in God can believe in odd events, but only people who believe in God can believe in miracles.

When the Red Sea parted, the Israelites did not say: "My, my! What an odd event." They said:

> I will sing to the Lord, for he has triumphed gloriously;
>   the horse and his rider he has thrown into the sea.
> The Lord is my strength and my song,
>   and he has become my salvation.
>
> (Exodus 15:1-2*a*)

When Jesus healed the paralytic, the crowd did not jump up and down and exclaim: "What a fluke! What an amazing event!" They did not even exclaim: "What a magician." The story says: ". . . they were all amazed and glorified God . . ." (Mark 2:12).

Even today two people can look at an extraordinary event and one can say, "Look at what happened!" and the other can say, "Look what God has done!" If the extraordinary event was helpful to someone, the nonbeliever can say, "Thank goodness" (which is a hedge), and the believer can say, "Thank God."

So if we are to look for miracles in the biblical sense, it is not enough for us just to look for amazing events. They have to be amazing events which can be attributed to the working of God.

What Makes a Miracle a Miracle?

What makes an amazing event more than an amazing event? What makes an amazing event a miracle?

Miracles, in the biblical stories, have a kind of *personal* quality about them. They are the kind of amazing events of which one can say, "Someone did that," instead of just saying, "That happened." It is a little hard to be very rigorous about the difference, but we can give some hints.

In the Bible, miracles are personal because they seem to have a kind of *purpose*. If a wandering Israelite had been standing at the edge of the Red Sea, saw the sea open leaving a great swath of dry land, and then sometime later saw the sea close again, even if Moses was waving his wand at the time, he would probably have said, "Isn't that something?" not "Isn't that a miracle?" But when the same Israelite saw the sea open for an escaping people, a people who were trying to worship and serve the Lord, saw the sea close on the pursuing enemy, then he said, "Ah, a miracle."

In the New Testament stories, if Jesus had gone around levitating houses or leveling mountains for the sheer joy of it, it is doubtful that anybody would have thought he was anything more than the leading magician of his time. But when they saw purpose in what he did—a healing, forgiving purpose, so that the blind saw and the sinner who was paralyzed walked—then they said, "Now that's a miracle," and glorified God.

Furthermore, miracles in the Bible seem to evoke a sort of *awe,* and awe is something different from surprise or astonishment; it seems a lot like reverence. One who experiences awe sees an event as an act and looks for the Actor (or sometimes for the Author of the whole play). We can all feel the difference, though it is hard to explain very precisely. Paint splashed on the rug may evoke amazement; paint spread properly on a canvas evokes awe. A loud noise can be surprising; the last movement of Beethoven's Ninth Symphony is awesome. In the New Testament, especially, the onlookers are continually filled with awe at what they see, and the presence of awe is a good clue to the personal quality which separates a miracle from an amazing event.

Also, miracles in the Bible sometimes call for some kind of *response* on the part of the beholder or on the part of the one who is healed by the miracle. One of the best examples is Mark 5:1-20, where the demoniac who is healed is told to go home and tell everybody what has happened to him. In Luke 5:1-11, the disciples who behold the miraculous catch of fish are told to follow Jesus. Those who watch miracles tend to get caught up in them; spectators who watch the divine drama suddenly find themselves thrust onto the stage with a role to play. People can stand amazed at magic or accident; after a miracle they are often asked to stand *for* something, to get involved.

All this is to say again that miracles are a very personal matter. They reflect the wishes of God who performs them. Probably most often only those who believe that God is doing things can perceive his actions. But sometimes people may look at events and suspect that they are actions. They may notice that the sea has parted and ask who did it; they may discover that their eyes are opened and want to thank someone.

Do Miracles Ever Happen?

The trouble with miracles is that they do not seem to fit very well into our way of looking at the world. We are largely convinced that the world operates according to fixed principles, scientific laws; events occur in accordance with these laws. If we hear that a scientific law has been "violated," we are inclined not to believe it. At the very least, that assumption makes us skeptical that miracles happen anymore. More likely it makes us skeptical that miracles ever happened. The reason that people in biblical times *thought* that miracles happened, we suspect, is that they simply did not know enough about scientific laws, did not realize that in the end there is a perfectly rational explanation for everything.

Sometimes, though, this "modern" way of looking at the world presupposes an odd view of a scientific "law." We think of a scientific law as being something like a traffic law: a car must stop at a red light. No one or no event is supposed to violate that law because it is against the rules; if anyone does violate the law, he is in for his share of punishment. But of course scientific laws are not "laws" in that sense at all. They are not really rules for the way things *must* behave; they are hypotheses which enable us to predict the way things will *probably* behave. They are not used to keep the universe in line (the way traffic laws are used to keep traffic in line). And if an event does not "obey" a scientific law, if something does not behave as predicted, we do not punish the offender; rather we revise the law. Scientific laws (or better, scientific hypotheses) are useful in proportion to their accuracy in enabling us to predict what will happen.

Some "laws," like the law for the force of gravity $F = G \left\{ \dfrac{m_1 m_2}{r^2} \right\}$, are tremendously accurate—that is, they enable us to predict the behavior of bodies in a wide range of instances. Other hypotheses are much more specialized and susceptible to a variety of exceptions. We try to work the exceptions into the hypotheses so that they will be more accurate tools for prediction.

Now all this is to say that we cannot really talk about people (or events) violating scientific laws the way we can talk about drivers violating traffic laws. Suppose, to take a very simple "scientific" hypothesis, we want to say that "everything which goes up comes down" and then discover that if a projectile is shot from the earth at sufficient velocity it does not come down (very soon at least) but goes into orbit around the earth. We do not say that the projectile has violated the law, but we simply revise the law: "Everything which goes up must come down, unless it goes up at a sufficient velocity to remain up." Then, of course, we try to purify the hypothesis: "What velocity is required for an object to go into orbit? What other hypotheses can we devise which will enable us to predict the conditions under which things which go up will not come down?" The point is not really so much to discover the rules which govern the universe, in the way that a new citizen tries to understand the laws which govern the United States. The point is to make our predictive capacity more and more sophisticated so that we will be able to predict with greater and greater probability what is going to happen next.

Furthermore, the principle of the so-called uniformity of nature, the idea that events will continue to occur as they have always occurred, that what goes up will continue to come down, is, of course, itself unprovable. If someone wants to prove that things will continue to occur as they have always occurred, we can only ask how he knows; and he can only answer, because they always *have* occurred that way, which is precisely the core of the problem.

Now it is sometimes held that the belief in the uniformity of nature is a faith, and that the scientists are really exercising a kind of faith when they make predictions. Whatever kind of faith it is, however, it is not the kind of faith which the Christian talks about when he talks about radical trust. The scientist assumes that his hypotheses will continue to "work" or at least to be adjustable within a reasonable range of probability, because it is this assumption which makes science useful and possible. This assumption might all fall apart someday (though I am not holding my breath), but if it does, science will all fall apart. The scientist does not necessarily believe in this great principle of the uniformity of nature, but the business of science is to make hypotheses, test them, and revise them. So the scientist goes about his business, usually without raising questions about this or that great principle.

This understanding of scientific law has implications for our understanding of miracles, because it gets less and less clear what makes a miracle a miracle if by miracle we mean an event that "violates" a scientific "law." If scientific laws are hypotheses which can be revised and sophisticated on the basis of apparent exceptions and which deal in probabilities rather than certainties, it is not clear at all what would count as a violation of a scientific law.

To take a very simpleminded example, suppose that one first-century scientific law, or hypothesis, was that people who are blind from birth do not gain their sight. Now a scientist who found himself in the first century might have studied hundreds of case histories of people blind from birth and discovered that in no case did anyone blind from birth ever receive sight. (John 9:32, indeed, assumes such an hypothesis.) Therefore he stands rather sure of his hypothesis—until one day he happens along just as Jesus happens along, and they both encounter a particular man who was blind from birth; and, by some means or other, Jesus gives the man his sight. Now the scientist would not say, "My law has been violated!" He would say, "I must revise my hypothesis," and he would come up with an hypothesis with greater predictive power, such as: "People who are blind from birth do not gain their sight unless Jesus somehow heals them."

If he was a sophisticated scientist, he might not be very happy with that hypothesis, because he would suspect that other exceptions might pop up and he would continually have to revise his hypothesis to include exceptions like: unless Jesus heals them;

or unless Paul heals them; or unless Peter heals them; or unless they pray fervently under unusual circumstances. By the end of a list of these kinds of exceptions, the hypothesis is not very helpful anymore; you never know when a new exception will pop up. So the scientist tries to find ways to generalize the hypothesis: what is it about Jesus, about the situation, about the man blind from birth which might be generalized so that the hypothesis would be useful in predicting the widest possible range of circumstances?

The process could go on indefinitely, and there would be no point at which the scientist would have to stop and say, "Ah, now a scientific law has been broken!" All he needs to say is, "Time to revise my hypothesis."

Therefore it is probably not very helpful to say that miracles are violations of scientific laws, because that definition of miracles really misinterprets scientific law, and it may misinterpret miracles, too.

Perhaps miracles are not really events which violate scientific laws. Perhaps miracles are events which are susceptible to two different kinds of explanation. One kind of explanation is "objective": it tries to show how the event fits the hypothesis which science uses to make predictions. The other kind of explanation is "personal": it relates the miracle to other kinds of hypotheses, hypotheses about the way God deals with people and the way people are supposed to respond.

It is not that one explanation is true and the other false; it may be that the explanations function differently, that one kind of explanation is valuable for one purpose and the other kind of explanation is valuable for another purpose.

Suppose, for example, the scientist discovers that there is a remarkable correlation between electric activity in a certain corner of the brain and the behavior commonly described as "falling in love." It may be that he could work out a device to discover whether there was unusual activity in that corner of the brain and from that be able to predict other physiological features, such as faster heart beat and sweaty palms. He might even be able to predict certain kinds of behavior—a propensity for being tongue-tied and an inordinate affinity for daydreaming. One way to "explain" what was going on with the subject of this study would be to say that he had such and such activity going on in such and such a corner of his brain.

But if our friendly subject wished to explain his odd behavior to his beloved, it would probably not be helpful to his cause were he to say, "My dear, such and such activity is now going on in such and such a corner of my brain." It would be far more appropriate to say, "I love you."

Now, this does not mean that one explanation is accurate and the other inaccurate; it means that one explanation is useful for some things (predicting sweaty palms) and the other explanation is useful for other things (candlelight, courtship, and delight).

It may be that some day the "scientific" outlook will so rule our society that one of us might say to another, "The protons in such and such a part of my brain are vibrating," and the other would respond longingly, "Mine, too," and romance would be underway. But I doubt it and hope not.

Understanding brain waves is useful for predictability; it is not useful for poetry, spontaneity, making love.

Perhaps (as we have already suggested) there are other events susceptible to two kinds of interpretation, the one "scientific" and the other "personal." Suppose there had been a sophisticated psychologist present when Jesus healed the paralytic. Suppose he could explain that the paralysis was the result of severe guilt about the paralytic's childhood feelings of desire for his mother, that his defense was this psychosomatic paralysis, and that the "cure" came when Jesus convinced him that he no longer needed to feel the guilt about his sexual urges. (I leave it to the scientists whether that counts as a scientific explanation; at least we are not at the point yet where we can reduce desire for mother and guilt to brain wave charts and release from guilt to a certain kind of electrical stimulation set in motion by the soothing sound of Jesus' voice.) Well, maybe so; the Christian does not really have to deny that explanation to have his miracle. Indeed such an explanation could be useful (has proved useful) to counselors of all sorts in trying to deal with those who are burdened with guilt.

However, that explanation does not get at one crucial question. What about the guilt? Is there any reason why the man should not feel guilty about his desire for his mother? And if he should not feel guilty about his desire for his mother, what in the world is to be done about it?

An alternative (not a contradictory) explanation of what happened to the paralytic is that it was a miracle, not just the miracle that a paralytic got up and walked, which the story itself makes clear is very much the subsidiary miracle, but the miracle that his sins were forgiven, were forgiven by Jesus. The "miraculous" explanation is that getting up and walking was all tied in with the fact that God in Jesus Christ forgave him altogether, that his guilt was objectively, actually wiped away, and that he did not need to feel guilty because there was no longer any reason to feel guilty.

Now heaven knows whether that kind of explanation would be of any help to the scientist in predicting what would happen to the next paralytic who comes his way. Presumably that kind of explanation was of immense help to this paralytic. It got him up out of bed. It was of immense help to the believers, who continued to tell the story, not as an example of a violation of a scientific law, but to proclaim that God in Jesus Christ forgives sins; not just the paralytic's sins, but other people's sins as well. That explanation is still "useful" to the preacher who can use the story to proclaim the forgiveness of sins to his congregation and can discover, to his own astonishment, guilt lifted and people formerly paralyzed physically or emotionally standing up and walking at last.

The explanation that what happened was the miracle of forgiveness does not rule out the scientist's explanation. The reference to miracle is probably not so precise, may not help predict such a wide range of cases, but it is somehow a *richer* explanation. It gives the person who accepts it, not only a new insight into the way the world works, but also a new sense of the way *he* works, a new sense of worth, commitment, freedom. The universe becomes, not an impersonal series of events guessed at by hypotheses, but the personal arena where God forgives sins. The person who accepts that explanation comes away not simply enlightened but redeemed.

To put it briefly, if not simply, miracles are not events which occur in violation of scientific laws (since it is almost impossible even to make sense of that definition). Miracles are events which are susceptible to alternative explanations, to objective explanations, and to personal explanations. It is not that one explanation is right and the other wrong, but that the different explanations serve different functions. The objective explanations may enable us to predict what is apt to happen under given circumstances and may enlighten us. The personal explanation may enable us to live under a variety of circumstances, may redeem us, or point to the one who does redeem us. Events *reduced* to science alone are like love reduced to brain waves, a thin gruel and small nourishment for the richness of our lives.

What About the Miracles in the New Testament?

Even if we want to admit that miracles are events which allow alternative explanations and that one explanation is that a miracle is an act of God, we are still left with the question of whether such miracles happened in New Testament times, whether there are any events which we at least would consider to be God's acts among people.

We can start by ruling out some unlikely options for interpreting the New Testament miracle stories. One option is the literalist option. The literalist wants to maintain that everything happened just as it is recorded. However, there are a number of problems with this approach. The nature of the sources makes it unlikely that events are recorded with any kind of scientific accuracy. Stories in the Gospels were passed on by word of mouth for years before they were written down, and inevitably embellishments crept in. Furthermore, as we have suggested, the Gospel writers were not reporters as much as they were theologians. They themselves did not try to produce with scientific accuracy the reports they had received. For instance, when Matthew is recording the story of the blind man on the road out of Jericho, he takes the one blind man of Mark's story, which was his source, and turns him into two blind men for his own theological purposes (Matthew 20:30; parallel, Mark 10:46-47). Historical accuracy was clearly not the point.

What is more, the people of New Testament times really did have a kind of prescientific understanding. Although a good deal of dubious prose has been written about our modern viewpoint, our way of looking at the world *has* changed. The first-century believer was not much concerned with proposing hypotheses, gathering evidence, testing cases. His world was still haunted by spiritual forces; demons and angels acted, and what was irregular was perhaps too quickly hailed as miraculous.

Moreover, if we are honest, we simply have to admit our own incredulity. It is hard for us to believe in Jesus walking on the water, loaves of fishes spectacularly multiplied, Lazarus returning from the grave. Whether our skepticism is a triumph of rationality or a failure of imagination, it is there as a given; we do not easily believe in the miraculous. We cannot simply take the stories at face value.

Another option which it is difficult for us to accept is the option proposed by the rationalists who seem to believe that everything happened much as it was recorded in the Gospels, but that there is a perfectly adequate, nonmiraculous explanation which is sufficient to understand what occurred. The Kellers, in their book *Miracles in Dispute,* quote a nice example of such rationalizing explanations by the eighteenth-century scholar Carl Friedrich Bahrdt:

> This, too, that Jesus walked on the sea and came towards the terrified Peter, who took him for a spirit—for this, too, there is more than one explanation with which one may be contented and whereby one may avoid the supernatural.
>
> The disciples' ship was near the shore during this event (John 6:21). Do you now find it impossible to believe that one or more pieces of timber lay on the shore or that one of these pieces of timber was floating in the water? May we not suppose that this piece of timber was by chance floating near the ship? We can easily imagine that Jesus, on the shore, might have seen this and Peter can easily be supposed to have overlooked it. We may well believe that Jesus, as the ship was near land, stepped on to the wood, felt that it bore his weight and approached the ship or boat on it, clambering in beside the disciples. Is it not easy to believe that the disciples, who never viewed anything clearly but always saw more than was really to be seen, were terrified by the figure whom they saw walking towards them, that Peter cried out, imagining a spirit and—that now the worthy folk passed on to the posterity the story of Jesus' journey on the hundred-ell cedar wood as if the waves themselves had borne up their master.[1]

Certainly all of us have heard sermons based on the Boy Scout version of the feeding of the five thousand—the idea that whoever provided the initial loaves and fishes for Jesus to bless inspired the stingy crowd to come forth with the bountiful supply they had been hoarding and to share generously one with another, a description which not only fails to take the text literally but also fails to take it seriously.

The problem, of course, is that when we seek steadfastly to "avoid the supernatural" we also tend to reduce the miraculous to the dull light of everyday. We may make the Bible "believable" by insisting that everything was in order, but we rob it of its power to show purpose, evoke awe, inspire commitment. It may be that

Jesus floated out on the board (though that strains credulity perhaps as much as the original story); if so we only have evidence that he was the earliest known surfer, and there is no touch of miracle, no sense that his activity was also the activity of a personal God. Miracles, we have suggested, are events which are susceptible to two kinds of explanation, objective and personal. The rationalists reduce them to the sort of event which can be exclusively explained in objective terms, and thus by explaining the miracle they really explain it away.

A third option is that of the radical form critics (particularly Rudolf Bultmann), who seem to hold that the miracle stories in the Gospels are a late, Hellenistic accretion to the originally purer Palestinian gospel, which dealt largely with Jesus as a preacher of the kingdom.

However, there are sayings in the Gospels which even the skeptical Bultmann accepts as being authentic sayings of the historical Jesus and which indicate that Jesus at least saw himself as a miracle worker. One is from Luke 11:20 (parallel, Matthew 12:28): "But if it is by the finger of God that I cast out demons, then the kingdom of God has broken in upon you."[2]

The second is from Luke 13:32: "Go and tell that fox: 'Behold, I am casting out demons and performing healings today and tomorrow, and on the third day I'll complete my task."[3]

If even the radical form critics admit that Jesus spoke of himself as an exorcist and miracle worker, and therefore performed miracles, it makes sense to assume that some of the miracle stories in the Gospels have their origins, not in later Hellenistic legends, but in the activities of Jesus himself.

Furthermore, not all the miracle stories in the Gospels look alike. Some stories, especially stories in the "apocryphal" Gospels do seem to have the elaborate detail of some of the Hellenistic miracle stories, such as those told about Apollonius of Tyana; but most of the miracle stories in the Gospels have a kind of simplicity and neatness about them which is very different from the form of the Hellenistic miracle tales. Indeed, one suspects that it is a theological suspicion of miracles rather than any very careful form criticism which causes men like Bultmann and Dibelius to suggest that the miracles are late and without historical grounding in the ministry of Jesus.

Two factors therefore move us toward a less skeptical historical evaluation of the miracle stories in the Synoptic Gospels. One factor is that the simplest explanation for at least some of the miracle stories is that they derive from miracles which Jesus actually did, since even Bultmann wants to admit that Jesus was a miracle worker, or at least an exorcist. The attempts of Bultmann, Dibelius, and others to find evidence that all the miracle stories arose only after the life of Jesus and in a Hellenistic milieu is finally unconvincing.

The second factor is a change in the way that most of us look at the world. We are not as convinced as earlier "modern" men and women that there is no place for the miraculous in a carefully ordered universe. Trite as it has become, Hamlet's reminder to Horatio is echoed by a number of people in our time, especially by younger people: "There are more things in heaven and on earth than are dreamt of in your philosophy." It is one thing to see the world as capable of sustaining hypotheses and revealing evidence; there is no backing off from that. It is another thing to see the world devoid of mystery and wonder; and a universe without wonder seems strangely pale even to so-called modern people.

Perhaps, therefore, we are more easily disposed to see some historical validity in the miracle stories of the Synoptic Gospels. A few principles may be useful in trying to discover what historical validity there is in the synoptic stories.

1. It is generally agreed by scholars that Mark's is the earliest Gospel, so if we are looking at traditions included in Mark, Matthew, and Luke, Mark's Gospel *usually* provides the earliest version of that tradition.

2. Furthermore, we have seen that the evidence of the sayings indicates very strongly that Jesus performed exorcisms, and so there is at least some reason to think that the exorcism stories may be those which have the greatest claim to historical validity. Indeed at some points it looks as though other miracle stories have been shaped to fit the form of exorcism stories, and we can suggest that the closer the story is to an exorcism story in formal characteristics and content, the clearer evidence we have that it may have some historical validity.[4]

Of course any attempt to get at the historical background for the miracle stories must admit that the passage of time and the theological concerns of the early church and of the Gospel writers would easily and almost inevitably shift the focus of the stories away from any concern with historical accuracy. The Gospels were not written primarily to be history; they were written to evoke faith. To get at the historical basis for the Gospels, we need sometimes not just to get at the Gospels but to get behind them as well. We can therefore suggest that the slighter the theological and confessional emphasis in the story the more likely it is to have historical validity (for example, the story of the healing of Peter's mother-in-law in Mark 1:29-31 seems to be told almost entirely out of biographical interest and lacks any clear theological or confessional point).

Of course even when we have raised the question of the historicity of the miracle story, we still must ask whether the story is the story of a *miracle*. In light of all that we have said about what makes a miracle a miracle, we can say that those stories which most fully suggest the *purposes* of God, those stories which evoke not mere astonishment but awe, which demand commitment, and which confront us with the reality of a personal and loving God are much more likely to have been real miracles—the kind of deeds we would expect of the God who came close to us in Jesus Christ.

All of this suggests an answer to the question with which we began: do miracles ever happen, and particularly, did miracles happen in the time of Jesus; are the stories in the Gospels stories of real events? Our answer would be that miracles *do* happen, if by this we mean that there are events which admit of two ex- planations, one objective and one personal. Further, such events certainly did happen in the ministry of Jesus, and probably some of the miracle stories in the Synoptic Gospels at least reflect the church's memory of such events.

What made the miracles important, however, and what makes them important for us, is not how odd they were but how personal they were, how much they revealed of who God was and what he was doing, and how much they pointed the way to a life enriched and enlivened by his grace.

CHAPTER 2

Miracles
in
the
Gospels

Although we shall pay some attention to the question of the historical validity of some of the individual miracle stories in the Gospels, we must recognize from the start that the question of historical validity is never the central concern of the Gospel writers themselves.

This is partly because the historical validity of the accounts is never really questioned in the Gospel narratives. Since the purpose of the Gospel writers is not to write history as we understand history, they do not take it upon themselves to raise questions of historical accuracy. They do not adduce evidence or cite witnesses for what they report (with a few exceptions, especially in regard to resurrection narratives; see John 21:24). Luke, as we shall see, comes the closest to trying to write "history," but even for him it is a history highly colored by theology and faith. Certainly the Gospel writers did not share the incredulity of our contemporaries when confronted with stories about miracles. Miracle stories abounded in the early centuries of our era, and the skeptics who demanded evidence were rare.

Furthermore, the miracles are explicitly *not* used as historical "proofs" of Jesus' special divine status. The idea that miracles in themselves, without interpretation, can simply be told as evident proofs of Jesus' unique role is rejected throughout the Gospels.

In the temptation stories in Matthew 4:1-11 and Luke 4:1-13, Jesus rejects miracles either as a response to his own personal needs or as a spectacular sign to convince unbelievers.

In Mark's Gospel Jesus adamantly refuses to give his opponents any "sign," any miraculous proof of his special status.

> The Pharisees came and began to argue with him, seeking from him a sign from heaven, to test him. And he sighed deeply in his spirit, and said, "Why does this generation seek a sign? Truly, I say to you, no sign shall be given to this generation" (Mark 8:11-12).

In Matthew and Luke the only sign which Jesus offers is the sign of Jonah. This probably originally referred to Ninevah's repentance which stands in opposition to the obdurateness of Jesus' own hearers (Matthew 12:38-42; Luke 11:29-32). In John's Gospel, though the use of "signs" is somewhat more varied (as we shall see), it is nevertheless clear that Jesus rejects miracles, or signs, as "proofs" of his unique relationship to God. He rather insists that true faith must be, not in his spectacular deeds, but in his person:

> They said to him, "Then what sign do you do, that we may see, and believe you? What work do you perform? Our fathers ate manna in the wilderness; as it is written, 'He gave them bread from heaven to eat.'"

> Jesus said to them, "I am the bread of life; he who comes to me shall not hunger, and he who believes in me shall never thirst'" (John 6:30-31, 35).

Indeed, as early as the earliest Gospel, it is clear that miracles are not told simply for their own sake, but because they have some special, theological meaning which the reader is to understand. In a curious episode in Mark 8, Jesus has been talking about the "leaven" of the Pharisees and the "leaven" of Herod and reminds the disciples of his own feeding miracles:

> "Are your hearts hardened? Having eyes do you not see, and having ears do you not hear? And do you not remember? When I broke the five loaves for the five thousand, how many baskets full of broken pieces did you take up?" They said to him, "Twelve. . . ." And he said to them, "Do you not yet understand?" (Mark 8:17b-21).

I confess that *I* don't yet understand,[1] but it is at least clear that as early as Mark's Gospel, even the most straightforward miracle stories are not being told simply for their own sake, but because they have a special, hidden significance.

Miracle stories, therefore, are told for a variety of theological purposes. Their meaning is as important as the claim that they took place. They always point beyond themselves to who God is, who Jesus is, or what we are supposed to be.

Having said that, we can now look at the Four Gospels to see what theological meaning miracles have in the work of the four Gospel writers, pausing from time to time to see what kind of historical validity can be credited to the accounts.

Miracles in the Gospel of Mark

While it is always dangerous to try to spot an emerging scholarly consensus before it actually emerges, there seems to be an emerging scholarly consensus that Mark did not simply come upon all of his miracle stories piecemeal but relied at some points at least on a pre-Markan miracle source.[2]

Mark's use of a miracle source

My own analysis of such a "source" suggests that it consisted primarily of exorcism stories or of miracle stories which were modeled after exorcism stories (e.g. Mark 4:35-41).

These stories are primarily the stories of a power struggle between the forces of the kingdom of God and the forces of the kingdom of evil (sometimes the forces of Satan, sometimes demonic forces). There is a saying of Jesus in Matthew 12:28 which seems to provide a valid interpretation of these pre-Markan miracle stories: "If it is by the Spirit [Luke, "finger"] of God that I cast out demons, then the kingdom of God has come upon you."

In these stories, Jesus' miraculous activity in casting out demons is not simply a kind of "sign" pointing to the kingdom; Jesus' activity is itself a victory in the establishment of the kingdom. Whenever Jesus speaks the strong word which sends the demons packing, God's powers have won another skirmish in the war against satanic powers. The kingdom is that much closer to its final triumph. Jesus is uniquely, but not exclusively, the one in whom God's kingdom is winning its victory. Thus from our very earliest sources on, miracles are not told simply as stories of amazing incidents, but as events in God's establishment of his reign in history.

Furthermore, in Mark's sources the exorcism stories often end with a call or a request to "be with" Jesus (see Mark 5:1-20; 3:7-15;

9:38-41; Luke 9:49-50). It seems that the call to "be with" Jesus was a call to join him in the power struggle for the kingdom. Those called to "be with" Jesus were called to join him in casting out demons and to become his fellow workers in the harvest of the kingdom (see Matthew 12:30).

Therefore, in these earliest pre-Markan stories, miracles were performed as part of God's battle to establish his kingdom, and they served as the focal point for recruiting new troops to join in that struggle, to "be with" Jesus.

We can look at three specific examples of the use of miracles in the sources which preceded Mark.

The Beelzebul controversy in Mark 3:19b-30 certainly contains some very early, pre-Markan material. (There is a somewhat different version of some of the same material in the sayings and traditions behind Matthew and Luke.)

The scribes recognize that what is involved in Jesus' miracles is the struggle between spiritual powers, but they fail to perceive which power Jesus represents:

> The scribes who came down from Jerusalem said, ". . . by Beelzebul . . . the prince of demons he casts out the demons." And he [Jesus] called them to him, and said to them in parables, "How can Satan cast out Satan? If a kingdom is divided against itself, that kingdom cannot stand. And if a house is divided against itself, that house will not be able to stand" (3:22-25).

Jesus' reply depends in part on an Aramaic pun. "Beelzebul" apparently means "Lord of the dwelling" and Jesus responds by saying, "If a dwelling is divided against itself, that dwelling will not be able to stand."

The whole story makes clear that Jesus' miracles take place in the context of a struggle, hostile powers arrayed against each other. Since it is the forces of Satan which Jesus is driving out, it cannot be Satan whom he serves. He must be on the side of the other great force in the power struggle, on the side of God himself. His exorcisms are not satanic magic tricks; they are victories for the kingdom of God. Even the use of the term "kingdom" in the phrase, "If a kingdom is divided against itself, that kingdom cannot stand," suggests the division of the world into two great realms, Satan's realm and God's. Jesus reminds the listener that he is at work overcoming the kingdom of Satan so that the kingdom of God may come to its final triumph.

The story of the exorcism in the synagogue (1:21-28) has been revised by Mark to represent some of his own theological concerns, but with a little effort we can reconstruct the pre-Markan form of the story.[3]

> There was a man with an unclean spirit; and he cried out, and said: "What have you to do with us, Jesus of Nazareth? I know who you are, God's holy one."
> Then Jesus rebuked him and said: "Shut up and come out of him." Then the unclean spirit convulsed him, and cried out in a loud voice, and came out of him.
> And all were amazed, so that they questioned with one another, and said: "Who is this, since he gives orders to unclean spirits and they obey him?" (See 1:23-27).

Though the evidence of a power struggle as the context for miracles is perhaps less obvious here, it is nonetheless as pervasive as in the Beelzebul controversy.

As comparison with non-Christian exorcism stories indicates, the little dialogue between the demons and Jesus is really a spiritual wrestling match over the soul of the demoniac.

The demon cries: "What have you to do with us [not just with the one demon, but with the whole demonic realm],[4] Jesus of Nazareth? I know who you are, God's holy one!" This is, first, an attempt to ward off Jesus ("What have you to do with us?" which means, "Don't mess with us, Jesus!"). Second it is an attempt to get Jesus under the demon's control by reciting Jesus' name and function: "I know who you are, God's holy one!" The *name*, of course, had great meaning and power for the Jewish people. That is why they would never speak the name of God, lest that imply that they had power over him.

The struggle continues as Jesus *rebukes* the demon. The term "rebuke" occurs time and again in these exorcism and miracle stories, and it represents a strong, effective, powerful word against the forces of sickness and evil. Jesus brings the full force of the power of God's word to bear against the demonic attempt to control *him* as well. The content of the rebuke is the forceful and pointed, "Shut up and come out," which is about as polite as it sounds. It shows God's great impatience with evil forces, a kind of holy wrath. In these stories the holy wrath always wins; the demon comes out, and the man is healed. Another victory is won for the kingdom.

The miracle evokes a kind of faith. (Note that it does not really *require* faith on the part of the demoniac; he has given no indication of faith one way or the other. All we get is the word of the demon and Jesus' willingness to do battle against the demonic.) The amazed crowd says: "Who is this, since he gives orders to unclean spirits and they obey him?" In part, we can suspect, these stories were originally told in order to arouse just such a question in the listeners: "Who is this Jesus, anyway? Is he really the one through whom the kingdom of God is breaking in, since he seems able to outwit and outfight the minions of Satan's kingdom?"

We may add one final note on this story. It is striking how often in Mark's sources (and in Mark) it is the demonic forces who recognize Jesus. In terms of the traditional background out of which these stories come, we can see why that is so. Supernatural forces are able to recognize supernatural forces, whether good or evil. The demons know Jesus when they see him, and Jesus can recognize Satan at a glance, however hidden the powers of each may be to the ordinary observer. Perhaps, as Bill Harrison has suggested, there is a more novel suggestion here as well. In Mark's Gospel (and perhaps in his sources) it seems to be the placid, plodding, ordinary types who never can get straight who Jesus is; the disciples believe only confusedly; the Pharisees believe not at all. Those who are at the farthest edge of respectability, the flagrantly sinful, the Gentiles, and especially those whom we would call mad can nevertheless perceive more clearly who Jesus is. Perhaps that is a hint that in Mark's sources those who look at the world with a prudent, careful, calculating objectivity will never be able to see what the mad and the anguished perceive at once. The mad and the anguished perceive that this man is no mere Galilean preacher, that his word and his deeds represent the power of God's kingdom breaking in on human history.

The demoniac of the tombs (5:1-20) was probably originally two stories, one of them part of the pre-Markan Christian tradition and one of them a Jewish folktale. The odd repetitions, the evident editorial devices, the shifts of emphasis all suggest that Mark has combined here two originally separate stories for his own theological purposes.[5]

The story which was in Mark's source probably read something like this:

They came to the other side of the sea. And when he had come out of the boat, there met him a man with an unclean spirit who lived among the tombs and had been bound with fetters and chains.

But the chains he wrenched apart, and the fetters he broke into pieces, and crying out with a loud voice, he said: "What have you to do with me, Jesus, Son of the Most High God? I adjure you by God, do not torment me!" But he rebuked him and said: "Come out of the man, you unclean spirit!"

And the spirit came out.

And they came to Jesus and saw the demoniac sitting there, clothed and in his right mind, and they were afraid. And those who had seen it told what had happened to the demoniac, and they began to beg Jesus to depart from their neighborhood.

(And as he was getting into the boat) the man who had been possessed with demons begged him that he might be with him. But he refused and said to him: "Go home to your friends, and tell them how much the Lord has done for you and how he has had mercy on you."

The central power struggle is still a key feature of this story. We have the demoniac's warding-off cry, his use of Jesus' name to try to control him. Jesus again responds by the strong word: "Come out of the man, you unclean spirit!"

We shall examine some of the theological implications of this story of possession and exorcism in the following chapter, but for now we can note that its original context apparently had to do again with an attempt to evoke a response of faith, now not on the part of the onlookers (who are mostly terrified) but on the part of the healed demoniac. The response of faith is now not simply the awestruck question: "Who is this?" but the more radical request to "be with" Jesus, that is, the request to be one of the small band of Jesus' close disciples. Jesus' response is a kind of missionary call, not a call to foreign missions but a call to home missions. The healed demoniac is sent to spread the good news in his own town, among his own people. The good news which he is to spread is, again, that in the activity of Jesus God himself is at work. If the distinction between magic and miracle is that a magic trick is simply a remarkable event and a miracle is a remarkable event which shows the mercy and purpose of God, then what the healed demoniac is to proclaim is that he has been healed by a miracle. The story is presumably told as an incentive to the listeners to accept the good news of God's miraculous activity in Jesus Christ and then to return to their homes and share that good news with their friends.

The historical validity of the miracle stories in Mark's source

It is impossible to establish with certainty the historical validity of any one of the miracle or exorcism stories, much less the validity of any particular detail of the story. However, there is evidence that some of these stories have a very early origin and may indeed go back to the teaching of the community around Jesus in the time prior to his crucifixion and resurrection.

At the very least, we can say that some of these exorcism stories represent a pre-Markan tradition, sometimes (as in the case of the Beelzebul controversy) a rather long and complicated tradition, which might indicate a rather long and complicated history. Mark has reshaped these stories in the service of his own theological interests.

Furthermore, in their original form, these stories betray interest in Jesus as exorcist, perhaps as a preacher of the kingdom, and as one who calls others to discipleship. They do not betray any particular interest in Jesus as the crucified and risen Lord. It is hard to imagine that any sizable portion of the tradition which arose *after* the crucifixion and resurrection could have been so devoid of concern with those central events of Christian faith.

Also, we have seen that there is almost incontrovertible evidence that in some of Jesus' authentic sayings he referred to himself as an exorcist and to exorcisms he had performed. Since it is clear that exorcism was an important part of his ministry, the simplest explanation for the origin of the exorcism stories is that they go back to that precrucifixion ministry of Jesus. Insofar as we can discern the theological position which underlies the telling of the exorcism stories, that position includes the claim that the kingdom of God is breaking in powerfully in Jesus himself and that people must choose for him or against him, for or against the kingdom. That is very like the view expressed in Jesus' parables, which most scholars have taken to be the earliest and most authentic representation of his own preaching and theology. If the exorcism stories represent the same kind of theology, they too may go back to the time of his ministry.

There is, therefore, good evidence that some of the miracle stories and particularly some of the exorcism stories which lie behind the Gospel of Mark have a very early date or origin, very likely a date which precedes the death and resurrection of Jesus.

The stories have changed and developed in the course of telling, and it is probably impossible to sort out for sure what is authentic detail and what is embellishment. At their heart, however, in their insistence that Jesus saw himself as being engaged in a great power struggle for God's kingdom against the kingdom of Satan, and in the call to the listeners to stand with Jesus against Satan, they represent a tradition with high claims to historical authenticity.

Jesus and those around him perceived what he was doing as casting out demons. They believed that his exorcisms represented victories for God's kingdom. Contemporary analysts might come up with alternative explanations of the same events, though that would not invalidate the reality of the events themselves. We have already suggested that the possibility of alternative explanations need not destroy our faith in miracles, and in the next chapter we shall look with greater care at the relationship of alternative explanations to the biblical talk about demons and exorcism.

Suffice it to suggest for now that, of course, it is a kind of faith which perceives a miracle when others may perceive magic or *mere* therapy. When faith sees a miracle, it does not see something *other* than what the skeptic sees; it sees something more. It sees that whatever else may be going on, God is at work in this particular activity. It sees that God's work moves toward the fulfillment of his kingdom. It sees, not just a remarkable event, but a splendid victory, one more skirmish won on the way to a final triumph. Such an explanation does not rule out the possibility of helpful alternative explanations, nor is it ruled out by such alternatives. It can enrich and be enriched by them. It proceeds in part from looking at the facts, but in part it proceeds from faith. Or, put another way, the events which evoke puzzlement or skepticism among some people evoke faith and commitment among others. Those others confess that whatever else is going on in Jesus' exorcisms, God's kingdom is breaking in there; and then they commit themselves to serving that kingdom.

Mark's own theology and the use of miracles

The following sketch of Mark's theological premises is very much my own. There are a number of alternative views of the thrust of Mark's theology, and you might want to look at Perrin's, Kelber's, Weeden's, Robinson's, or Marxsen's, as suggested in the bibliography and footnotes.

In my view, Mark's Gospel is a book of secrets; it contains special information which is revealed only to the insiders, to the community of faith.

There are places where this special concern for relating information to the insider is made explicit: "And what I say to you I say to all . . ." (13:37). "But when you see the desolating sacrilege set up where it ought not to be (let the reader understand) . . ." (13:14).

At other points the stress on special information for the reader is scarcely less evident: "He who has ears to hear, let him hear" (4:9). Sometimes it is clear that events, words, and actions have hidden meanings which are not immediately evident to the casual reader, as in the reference to the secret significance of the feeding miracle in 6:51-52.

> And he got into the boat with them and the wind ceased. And they were utterly astounded, for they did not understand about the loaves, but their hearts were hardened.

The rationale for secret information in Mark's Gospel is given in 4:11: "To you has been given the secret of the kingdom of God, but for those outside everything is in parables."

From a close reading of Mark's Gospel, we can get some clues to the nature of the secret or mysterious information which Mark wishes to impart to the alert and faithful reader.

Certainly one stress in Mark's Gospel is that the meaning of Jesus' role is to be discovered in his passion and death. Three times Mark has Jesus predict his own passion. This underlines the central importance of suffering and crucifixion in Jesus' mission (8:31; 9:30-32; 10:32-34). The climactic confession of faith in Mark's Gospel comes in the centurion's recognition at the cross: "And when the centurion, who stood facing him, saw that he thus breathed his last, he said, 'Truly this man was the Son of God!'" (15:39). The meaning of Jesus' sonship is revealed precisely in his suffering and death; that is one of the great secrets of Mark's Gospel.

The other great secret is also suggested in the three passion predictions which are, of course, also resurrection predictions. It has generally been thought that Mark does not have any place for the appearance of the risen Lord or for his activity in relation to the community of faith in his Gospel. The Gospel breaks off with the story of the empty tomb, and unlike the other three Gospels does not have any stories of the appearance of the risen Lord following the empty tomb narrative (see 16:1-8). The cryptic words spoken to the women at the tomb, "But go, tell his disciples and Peter that he is going before you to Galilee; there you will see him, as he told you" (16:7), is another of Mark's hints, not to the disciples, but to the reader.[6] It is a call to the reader to look at the "Galilee" section of Mark's Gospel (chapters 1-10) in order to "see" the risen Lord. There are no appearance stories at the end of Mark's Gospel because the entire first section of the Gospel is a revelation of the way in which the living Lord continues to relate to the community of faith. (There has been wide agreement that Mark's Gospel includes a "Galilee" section and a "Jerusalem" section and that somehow Galilee has an especially valuable place in Mark's theology; but the Galilean section of the Gospel has not generally been seen as the place where Mark shows the relationship of the risen Lord to the community of faith.)

Whatever one may do with the strange ending of Mark's Gospel, it seems reasonably evident that the opening chapters of Mark, including the miracle stories, do not merely tell the story of Jesus' ministry out of historical curiosity, but insist that Jesus continues to be active in the life of the community of faith. So, for instance, the story of the paralytic and the authority to forgive sins in Mark 2:1-12 is not just a story about an argument Jesus had during his ministry. It is a story which validates the church's authority to pronounce the forgiveness of sins in the name of its living Lord. Similarly, other stories in Mark reflect the community's ongoing relationship to Christ. This relationship is reflected in several themes.

One theme is faith versus fear. The community is called to faith in the living Lord, in Jesus. It can respond either by being faithful or by being fearful, which is the opposite of faithfulness. This theme is evident in such passages as 5:36, Jesus' word to Jairus, "Do not fear, only believe," and in the exhortation in the story of walking on the water, "Take heart . . . have no fear" (6:50). Even at the end of the Gospel, when the women hear the word that Jesus is risen, they respond not with faith, but with fear (16:8).

Another theme which reflects the relationship of the living Lord to Mark's community is the theme of the mission to the Gentiles. Clearly one of the great debates in the early church was whether the Gospel was to be preached to Gentiles as well as Jews. Mark strongly supports the Gentile mission (he writes presumably for

Gentiles) and uses the authority of Jesus to support that mission. This is most evident in the story of the Syrophoenician woman in 7:24-30; but it is clear elsewhere, also, that the "risen" Lord authorizes the mission to the Gentiles. As several scholars have noted, part of the importance of Galilee in Mark's Gospel seems to be that he sees it as the starting point for the Gentile mission; there was a large Gentile population there, and theologically it provides for Mark the place where the Gentile mission can be carried out.[7]

A third theme, which reflects the relationship of the living Lord to Mark's community, is the theme of Jesus' authority.

Mark's Gospel is not motivated by historical curiosity but by living faith, and when he insists on Jesus' authority to forgive sins (2:1-12) or his authority over the sabbath (2:28) he is not talking about Jesus' authority *back then,* but about his ongoing authority, vested in the church, which is now empowered to pronounce the forgiveness of sins and to exercise freedom from sabbath regulations.

The living Lord, therefore relates to Mark's community by calling people to faith (and people respond either with faith or with fear), by authorizing the mission to the Gentiles, and by declaring his authority and vesting authority in the church which serves him as Lord.

Some miracle stories in Mark

With these themes in mind, we can now look at the way in which Mark's telling of some of the miracle stories reflects some of his own theological concerns.

Mark 1:23-28. The exorcism in the synagogue. Mark takes a typical exorcism story with its stress on Jesus' power struggle against the demons and adds his own particular emphases. Verse 27 includes what is almost certainly a Markan phrase: "A new teaching! With authority." What Mark wishes to stress in the story is not Jesus' power to cast out demons, but his authoritative teaching, which stands out radically against the authority of the synagogue where the miracle takes place (and where the demoniac has thus far found no healing).

There is one other trace of Mark's editorial work in this story. We should perhaps translate 1:28, not "and at once his fame spread everywhere throughout all the surrounding region of Galilee," as the RSV does, but rather "and at once his fame spread everywhere

throughout all the region which surrounded Galilee."[8] For Mark
the territory around Galilee is Gentile territory, and it may be that
Mark is here using an exorcism story to stress the warrant of the
Gentile mission, to insist that Jesus' authority can extend beyond
the boundaries of the Jewish territory to reach Gentiles as well.

Mark 5:1-20; 7:24-30. Taking the Gospel from "insiders" to
"outsiders." The story of the demoniac of the tombs is rich in
theological implications, some of which we shall discuss in the
following chapter. Mark's purpose in telling the story, however,
seems to be once again to show that Jesus as Lord of the church
validates the mission to the Gentiles. Originally this was apparently
two stories, one a story about Jesus and the demoniac of the tombs,
one a Jewish folktale about an exorcist who drove the demons into
the swine and sent them to their death. (Swine of course were
unclean animals, and were owned by Gentiles; the story is really a
tall tale in which a clever Jewish exorcist outwits the demons and
also provides a cautionary lesson to the Gentiles on the dangers of
raising unclean animals.) Mark has combined the original "Christian" story of Jesus' miracle with the story of the swine in order to
move the exorcism story into Gentile territory (the country of the
Gerasenes and the Decapolis.) When Jesus sends the healed
demoniac home to tell what the Lord has done, he sends him to the
Decapolis, which was Gentile territory, and thus validates the
preaching of the Gospel to non-Jews.

There is one other sign of Mark's theological concerns in the
ending of this story. As the story was originally told, when Jesus
urges the healed man to go home and "tell what the *Lord* has
done," he presumably means what Yahweh, God, has done. Mark
reinterprets the command from his side of Easter, from the faith
that Jesus is the living Lord, and has the healed demoniac go home
and tell what *Jesus* has done. Jesus is seen (from Mark's side of
resurrection) to be the very Lord (5:19-20).

The story of the Syrophoenician woman in 7:24-30 also reflects
Mark's concern with the Gentile mission. Jesus' insistence on saving
the bread for the children (the Jews) certainly reflects some of the
arguments of Jewish Christians in Mark's own day. When the
Syrophoenician woman convinces Jesus to change his mind, Mark
is able to argue against the Jewish Christians that Jesus himself
validates the mission to Gentiles and not just the mission to Jews.

Mark 5:21-43. Jairus' daughter and the woman with the

hemorrhage. Almost certainly Mark has fitted these two stories together to serve his own theological purposes. The common theme which links the stories is the theme of faith, and the fundamental point of the stories is summed up in 5:34: "Your faith has made you well."

As we have seen, the call to faith is contrasted with the temptation to fear in 5:36. Furthermore, the story, rather like the story of Lazarus in John 11, is in part a story of the meaning of Jesus' power as the resurrected one, as the one who gives life. There are many indications that Jesus here is life-giver. Jairus' plea is that Jesus should come and touch his daughter, "so that she may be made well, and live" (5:23). Two different terms are used to describe the girl's healing, both of which, elsewhere, are terms for rising after death (5:41, 42). The girl is not just healed; she is resurrected. Those who witness the scene are Peter, James, and John who in Mark's Gospel are witnesses to the mystery of resurrection.[9] The response to the healing is expressed in terms appropriate to a story of raising the dead. Mark writes that the onlookers were "overcome with *amazement*" *(ekstasis)*. This term occurs only one other time in Mark's Gospel, in 16:8 where the women who find the empty tomb, the sign of Christ's own resurrection, flee "for trembling and *ekstasis* had come upon them." The whole story of Jairus' daughter and the woman with the hemorrhage, therefore, seems to be a call to faith in Jesus' healing power, but more than that in the life-giving power of Jesus the risen Lord.

There is another important motif in these two stories, suggested by Kathy Johnson. In both of these instances Jesus shows great compassion for women, and particularly for women who are in a state of cultic uncleanness, the one with a blood flow, the other presumed to be dead. By not only healing but touching both of these women, Jesus stands fundamentally against the cultural and religious barriers which his society tried to raise against women, and insists that the gifts of healing and life, the love of God, and the affirmation of human worth are as available to women as they are to men.

Mark 9:14-29. The "epileptic" boy. Mark again appears to combine two different stories. One of the stories is preserved largely intact in Luke 9:37-43*a*, so it is fairly easy to see what features Mark has added: (1) There is the expression of awe in the presence of Jesus as he returns from the Mount of Transfiguration (9:15). (2) The scribes are present (9:14). (3) There is the whole scene with the father, including the second description of the illness and the discussion of faith. (4) The description of healing is strikingly different from that used in Luke. In Luke Jesus "heals" the boy, in Mark he "raised" the boy, and the boy "arose," (the same two terms in the same order as in Mark 5:41-42). So, too, in Mark only, the boy becomes "like a corpse," so that the crowd says, "He is dead." (5) Mark adds the saying on prayer in 9:29.

As in the story of Jairus' daughter, Mark has taken a miracle story from his tradition and changed it in such a way that it becomes a testimony to the life-giving power of the living Lord. The awe with which Jesus is greeted is appropriate as a response to the living Lord as he comes from the Mount of Transfiguration, where the meaning of resurrection is conveyed to Peter, James, and John. Jesus does not simply heal an epileptic, he raises one who is like a dead man. The proper response to Jesus is, as so often in Mark, the response of faith. The stress on the authority of the living Lord for his community is there in the contrast with the scribes and in the injunction to the disciples concerning the power of prayer.

A story which probably once bore testimony to the power of Jesus during his early ministry to do battle against the demons for the sake of the kingdom has become, in Mark's hands, a story of the authority of the risen Lord, who gives life, calls for faith, and continues to instruct his church.

Preaching on miracles in Mark

There have already been a number of homiletic hints contained in our interpretation of the specific passages, but perhaps we can bring some of these hints together in a more systematic form.

1. In Mark (as in the other Gospels) miracle stories are never told simply for their own sake or as proofs of Jesus' special status. Therefore faithful preaching of the miracles in Mark will require us to look carefully at the theological implications of the stories; not just at what may or may not have happened, but at what the events *mean*. (A cautionary note must be added; many of those in our congregations are concerned with whether or how miracles may have happened, and at some point, either in Bible study or as an introduction to a sermon, that issue must be honestly faced.)

2. Miracle stories in Mark are not just stories about what the

historical Jesus did and taught among the people of his time. They are stories about the relationship of the crucified and risen Lord to the church of Mark's time. Our preaching must grow out of some understanding of what Mark thought the risen Lord had to say to Mark's community; it must also grow out of the imaginative and faithful attempt to discern what the living Lord has to say to our communities.

3. Mark's insistence that his is a book of secrets or mysteries can at least serve to remind us that the biblical stories are told in faith and can be fully apprehended only in faith; there is always more here than meets the eye.

4. Some of the specific themes which are evident in Mark's theology seem to me to provide helpful clues for preaching today. (We shall talk about the special case of the demonic and exorcism as they are reflected in Mark's sources in the next chapter.)

Mark's Gospel is in large part a call to faith in Jesus as the one whose sonship to God is revealed precisely in his suffering death and in his resurrection. The miracle stories can often be preached as calls to choose between faith and fear, to accept the life-giving power of the crucified and risen Lord or to shrink back into anxiety and unbelief.

Mark's Gospel insists that Jesus' ministry and our ministry cannot be confined to the privileged insiders; for Mark, the privileged insiders were the people of Israel. We shall need to look at our own communities to see who those people are who seem to think they have a monopoly on grace. All too often, I suspect, we shall discover that our congregations are sure that the Gospel is somehow especially for them, and we have encouraged them in that assumption. Mark's Gospel calls us to see that mercy breaks down barriers and that the call to service cannot be limited by geographic, cultural, or economic barriers.

Mark's Gospel insists that Jesus' authority is still actively related to his community; that authority stands over against human sin and guilt and over against all human authority—political, cultural, or religious. The Son of Man is Lord over the sabbath; that is, his life-giving power is not limited by any human institution or prejudice, by religious scruples, by racial or sexual discrimination. His authority, and his authority alone, can make clear the meaning of our mission and can validate that mission.

5. Finally, and perhaps self-evidently, Mark's Gospel assumes

that God in Jesus Christ really is active in occasions of healing, freeing, giving life. It provides clues for us to discern the continuing activity of God in Jesus Christ wherever healing, freeing, and giving of life occur. It calls us to be engaged prayerfully and faithfully in ministries which heal people, set them free, and give them life (all of us who are Christians, of course, not just professional clergy). Preaching which is faithful to Mark is faithful to the belief that God is actively at work in his world and that we are to proclaim and cooperate in his activity. In other words, preaching which is faithful to Mark is faithful to the reality of miracles.

Miracles in the Gospel of Matthew

While we have to do some complicated guesswork in order to discover the source or sources of Mark's miracle stories, we know the source of Matthew's miracle stories. It was Mark. This means, for one thing, that we have an easier time discerning Matthew's special theological interests. We can see where and how he changed Mark and assume that those changes indicate his particular concerns. We can also assume that he *had* some interests different from those of Mark. After all, he and his congregation already had Mark's Gospel, so there was no point in simply retelling the stories in Mark. He must have had something additional he wanted to say, and that is why he redid the miracle stories as part of his Gospel. (We use "he" for Matthew without meaning to deny the possibility that Matthew may be the product of a "school" as suggested in Krister Stendahl, *The School of St. Matthew*. Philadelphia: Fortress Press, 1968.)

Matthew's theology

Matthew was almost certainly writing for a Jewish-Christian church (though not necessarily a church in Palestine) as Mark was writing for a Gentile church, so different themes become centrally important.

In Matthew's use of the miracle stories, two concerns are especially evident. First, miracles are used in Matthew to indicate the fulfillment of prophecy. One of Matthew's great concerns is to show the relationship between the Old and New Covenants and time and time again he takes some word or event in the ministry of Jesus and shows how it fulfilled the Old Testament prophecy. At two points, at the end of a series of miracle stories, Matthew quotes the Old Testament in interpreting the significance of Jesus' miracles:

> That evening they brought to him many who were possessed with demons; and he cast out the spirits with a word, and healed all who were sick. This was to fulfil what was spoken by the prophet Isaiah, "He took our infirmities and bore our diseases" (8:16-17).

And in 12:16 and following the so-called "messianic secret" of Mark is reinterpreted as a fulfillment of the prophecy of Isaiah 42:1-4.

Second, Matthew uses miracles as sermon illustrations. Matthew's Gospel is divided into five great sections; each section contains a sermon followed by some narrative material.[10]

Prologue: chapters 1-4.

Section I: 4:23-9:34 (on Jesus' authority). The Sermon on the Mount stresses his teaching authority; the following narrative illustrates his authority in working miracles and in disputes with the Jewish leaders.

Section II: 9:35-12:50 (on mission). The discourse warns the disciples that their fate will be like that of John and Jesus. The narrative illustrates the growing hostility to John and Jesus which is a warning to the disciples—that they can expect hostility, too.

Section III: 13:1-17:27 (secrets of the kingdom). The discourse presents the parables of the kingdom. The narrative shows how the people fail to understand the secrets of the kingdom which have been entrusted to the disciples.

Section IV: 18:1-20:34 (on church leadership). The discourse spells out the leaders' responsibility to the "little ones," who are the church members. The narrative shows Jesus' own concern for "little ones" and also points to the validity of the Gentile mission.

Section V: chapters 21-27:56. Here some of the narrative does foreshadow the following discourse section. The discourses of 23 and 24-25 point to the final judgment when the wrongdoers will be condemned and the righteous will be saved. The narrative which is the passion narrative shows that the days of judgment are already beginning in the ministry of Jesus.

Epilogue: The resurrection narratives, chapters 27:57-28.

Whereas Mark's Gospel is largely a book of secret information calling for faith, Matthew's Gospel is more a book of teaching calling for obedience. It may indeed have been a rule book for church leaders with the teachings (the five sermons) illustrated by the succeeding material. In traditional terms, Matthew is more didactic than kerygmatic.

In addition to the stress on Old Testament prophecy and the fivefold sections of sermon (or teaching) and illustration, we can discern other theological themes in Matthew.[11]

In Matthew, and particularly in the miracle stories, there is a "higher" Christology than in Mark. There is greater concentration on the person of Jesus and less concentration on the subsidiary figures in the miracle narratives.

The concern with faith which we saw in Mark is here further stressed and elaborated. Faith, which in Mark is sometimes the result of a miracle, here seems increasingly to be a prerequisite for miracle. Faith stands in contrast to the little faith of those who do not expect the miraculous (e.g., compare Matthew 8:26 with Mark 4:39 and the addition of the story of Peter to the walking on the water, Matthew 14:28-31).

There is a strong eschatological expectation in Matthew, but the kingdom is not so much an in-breaking kingdom as a future kingdom (see the parables of chapter 25). When the kingdom comes, it will be a time of judgment, with Jesus as judge separating the sheep from the goats.

The test by which sheep will be separated from goats is largely the test of obedience to the new and higher law which has come in Jesus. In Matthew's Gospel Jesus comes "not to abolish [the law] but to fulfil [it]" (5:17). In Mark the law is somewhat superseded by Jesus; in Matthew the law is expanded, illumined, elevated, but certainly not destroyed. Jesus presents a higher righteousness, and good works become the test of faithfulness (see 25:31-46).

Finally, the somewhat irreverent or at least ambivalent attitude which Mark's Gospel exhibits toward the original disciples is largely changed by Matthew to a more reverent view. So, for instance, in the discourse on the leaven, in Mark's Gospel the disciples never *do* understand (8:21); in Matthew they finally catch on (16:12). The disciples provide a model for Matthew's readers, who are called to discipleship.

In sum, then, Matthew writes for Jewish Christians, suggesting that Jesus brings a higher law which fulfills the old covenant. Christians look toward a final judgment when those who are obedient to the higher law will be blessed and those who are disobedient will be condemned.

Some miracle stories in Matthew

Matthew 8:1-4. The healing of a leper. Matthew takes this miracle out of the Markan order of events in order to make it the first of Jesus' miracles, the immediate "illustration" of the Sermon on the Mount which has gone before.

As the Sermon on the Mount compares Jesus' teaching authority to Moses' and shows Jesus as the new Moses who provides the higher Torah for God's people, so the cleansing of the leper shows that Jesus' miracle-working authority also puts him in closest correspondence to the expectations of the Mosaic law.

Whereas in Mark's Gospel the story is told in part to show Jesus' compassion for the leper, or his anger at leprosy (Mark 1:41), in Matthew's Gospel there is no emphasis on Jesus' emotions, only on his healing authority. When in Mark's Gospel the conclusion and point of the story really come in the leper's spreading of the news about Jesus, Matthew makes no mention of it, but points simply to the command to the leper to "offer the gift that Moses commanded, for a proof to the people." It is the proof of Jesus' active authority which forms the heart of the story for Matthew.[12]

Matthew 14:22-33. Walking on the water. We can perceive Matthew's special concerns by comparing his version of the story with that in Mark 6:45-52. For one thing, Matthew eliminates the difficult suggestion in Mark that Jesus had intended to pass the disciples by on his way across the sea (Mark 6:48). More important, Matthew adds the whole story about Peter's attempt to walk on the water, and thereby makes the miracle story a lesson on his favorite themes of faith, unfaith, and discipleship.

Peter, of course, is especially important in Matthew's Gospel (see 16:18-19), but beyond that he certainly represents here an example for Matthew's readers, caught between the faith which makes him willing to follow Jesus' bidding and the unbelief which causes him to doubt, hesitate, and start to sink. The point is summed up in Jesus' word to Peter, "You little-faith, why did you doubt (or hesitate)?" (see 14:31).

Matthew also enhances the drama of the miracle by adding beating waves to the strong wind (14:24). The disciples, who in Mark are utterly astounded and fail to understand, here "worshiped him, saying, 'Truly you are the Son of God'" (14:33). They are thus brought to faith by the miracle, providing, one supposes, an example which Matthew's readers are to follow. Their cry, "Truly you are the Son of God," is of course an instance of the heightened Christology of Matthew's miracle stories or at least an example of the heightened awareness of the disciples who behold the miracle.

Matthew 8:5-13. The centurion's servant. Here, unfortunately, Matthew has not used Mark so we cannot compare those two versions. Luke does have a version of the story, which presumably means that he and Matthew had some source in common, and we can therefore make some guesses about those touches in Matthew's story which represent his particular theological bent. Two themes which are common both to Matthew and Luke in the story are certainly congenial to Matthew's concerns elsewhere. One is the stress on authority; the centurion implicitly compares the authority under which he stands to Jesus' authority (8:9). Matthew underlines the importance of Jesus' authority in 7:29 and again at the very end of the Gospel (28:18), where the risen Lord says: "All authority in heaven and on earth has been given to me." The other theme common to Matthew and Luke which this story stresses is the theme of faith, here the faith of the centurion: "Truly, I say to you [says Jesus], not even in Israel have I found such faith" (8:10). Then Matthew underlines the theme as Luke does not, by having Jesus say to the centurion: "Go; be it done for you as you have believed" (or "had faith"; 8:13).

In Matthew's Gospel Jesus heals the centurion's servant strictly on the grounds of the centurion's faith; in Luke's Gospel the elders of the Jews present the centurion's set of credentials before Jesus can perform the miracle. In part this may represent Matthew's more radical stress on the saving power of faith apart from righteousness (in this instance at least). More likely Luke has taken the occasion for a little homily on the worth of the Romans, a theme to which he returns elsewhere in his writing.

Perhaps most characteristically, Matthew here inserts the saying, which Luke includes elsewhere, about the openness of the kingdom and the grounds for judgment:

"I tell you, many will come from east and west and sit at table with Abraham, Isaac, and Jacob in the kingdom of heaven, while the sons of the kingdom will be thrown into the outer darkness; there men will weep and gnash their teeth" (8:11-12).

This represents Matthew's strong concern with last judgment, the belief that the validation of the faithful will come at the end of time. It also represents his polemic against the Jews who have refused to believe in Jesus, and his confession that the gospel is now being received by Gentiles like the centurion.

Matthew 8:28-34. Those swine again. Here again we can compare Mark's version of the story (Mark 5:1-20) and see what changes Matthew has made.

We note for one thing how little concerned Matthew is with faithfully reproducing his sources. For some reason (in order to have twelve healings in this section of his Gospel, twelve being an important number?) Matthew feels called upon to double the number of demoniacs.

Second, in Matthew's story the focus is almost entirely on Jesus and not much at all on the demoniacs. The description of the demoniacs' illness is omitted. The people's fear is directed, not toward the demoniacs, but toward Jesus. Matthew omits the missionary charge which represents the conclusion and point of Mark's story. The stress is entirely on Jesus' healing authority.

Finally, Matthew adds the instructive phrase *"before the time,"* in verse 29. "Have you come here to torment us *before the time?"* (Dean Krister Stendahl has suggested the significance of this phrase.) Again Matthew places stress on the eschatological conclusion which lies ahead, when Jesus will return as judge and establish his final rule over the forces of evil. The exorcism is a preliminary sign of that victory and judgment which are yet to come. (In Mark the victory is already coming; the battle has been joined.)

Preaching on miracles in Matthew

Again we shall try to bring some suggestions together in more systematic form.

1. In Matthew's miracle stories the focus is less on the person to be healed than on Jesus himself. This emphasis is helpful if we want to preach on the person of Jesus, less helpful if we want to focus on the condition of those (of us) who need to be healed by him. The stories are less anecdotal, less dramatic, and in that sense

less fun to preach on than the miracle stories in Mark's gospel.

2. The focus in Matthew is particularly on Jesus' authority, an authority which corresponds to his role as the new Moses and which is exercised in fulfillment of Old Testament prophecy.

3. As in Mark there is a strong stress on faith, but here for the most part faith seems to be an absolute prerequisite for healing (or salvation). Of course in Peter's case it is part faith and part unfaith, but for the others the extent of their faith seems to be directly related to the extent of Jesus' willingness to work the miracle.

4. The note of final judgment hangs over Matthew's Gospel in the miracles as in other places. Jesus' authority and the believers' faith will receive a final vindication in the Last Day when Jesus returns as Judge.

5. The miracles, in part, show the fulfillment of the messianic prophecies of the Old Testament and show that the promises given to the Fathers are now fulfilled in Jesus. When we preach on the miracle stories in this way, we are really preaching Matthean theology.

Miracles in the Gospel of Luke

Unlike Mark and Matthew, Luke tells us explicitly why he writes his Gospel:

> Inasmuch as many have undertaken to compile a narrative of the things which have been accomplished among us, just as they were delivered to us by those who from the beginning were eyewitnesses and ministers of the word, it seemed good to me also, having followed all things closely for some time past, to write an orderly account for you, most excellent Theophilus, that you may know the truth concerning the things of which you have been informed (Luke 1:1-4).

The concern with an "orderly account" and with "eyewitnesses" makes it sound as if Luke is much more an historian than Mark or Matthew (though Luke may think that the eyewitnesses have passed on their tradition in Mark and his other sources. There is no evidence that he had contact with eyewitnesses in writing his Gospel. Acts is another matter.) So, too, the concern with knowing the truth stands over against Mark's demand for faith or Matthew's concern for right action, central themes in their Gospels. However, even for Luke the point is clearly not simply to present informational truth, but to present theological truth, saving truth, the truth about the way God acts in history.

Luke's theology[13]

Luke wrote a two-volume work, Luke–Acts, and we cannot really understand what is going on in one without understanding what is going on in the other. The very fact that Luke writes a two-volume work tells us something about his theological perspective. The ministry of Jesus has now become one stage of an ongoing history which will include the history of the church. Jesus' ministry, death, and resurrection are no longer the great eschatological events, the dawning of the kingdom. They initiate the time of salvation in a special way, but the history which begins in Jesus may move on for a long while before it reaches its consummation; the church no longer feels the eschatological pinch. For the first time in Christian theology, historical self-understanding emerges.

For Luke–Acts the meaning of history is not determined by the activity of people but by the acts of God; history is "salvation history." There are three great periods of God's activity with humankind. The first period is the period of preparation, the period of the prophets, up to and including John the Baptist. The second period is the period of Jesus, which is in a special way the time when God's activity reaches its fullness, the time when salvation is released within human history. The third period is the period of the Spirit, the period of the church, which begins at Pentecost, continues through Luke's day, and extends toward some indefinite future when God will finally bring the consummation of history. (There may be a kind of latent historical trinitarianism here: history is divided into the period of the Father, the period of the Son, and the period of the Holy Spirit.)

Within this general pattern of Luke's concern with salvation history, we can perceive several theological themes. Luke's Christology is more "subordinationist" than that of the other Gospels. Jesus is more a "divine man" and less God incarnate. Jesus prays a considerable number of times in Luke's Gospel (not just for show as in John 11:42), and there is no doubt that the Father has the central place in Lukan theology. Jesus also appears to be a kind of model for the apostles and the later church. Some of the terminology for his miracles is later used for theirs (as we shall see). Certainly in Luke, Jesus becomes the first Christian martyr; his prayer for forgiveness for his tormentors (23:34) and his pious final words, "Father, into thy hands I commit my spirit!" (23:46), stand in sharp contrast to Jesus' cry in Mark, "My God, my God, why hast thou forsaken me?" (15:34). Jesus' words are strikingly similar to Stephen's words in Acts 7:59-60. Both Jesus and Stephen serve as exemplars for the later Christian church. For Luke, Jesus is the founder of the church (see Luke 24:47-49; Acts 1:8), but having founded the church he ascends to heaven and leaves its everyday operation in the hands of the Holy Spirit (Acts 1:8-9). This contrasts with the presence of the risen Lord in the Matthean (I think the Markan) and sometimes in the Johannine material.

For Luke, the great act of cosmic eschatology is put off to an indefinite future. In the meantime, eschatology is individualized. Jesus tells the thief that on the very day of his death he will be with Jesus in paradise (23:43). At the moment of his death, Stephen sees the Son of Man (who traditionally is to come at the end of history, at the Last Judgment) standing to receive him immediately into heaven, and Stephen's final words are: "Lord Jesus, receive my spirit" (Acts 7:59). Since the kingdom's coming is now postponed, the primary virtue for Luke tends to be patience rather than risk and alertness. Faith becomes faith, not so much in the incredible future which is breaking in, but in the past events of Jesus' ministry. Instead of the kingdom we get the church; instead of the need for radical decision we get the need for acceptable church order under the apostles and authoritative doctrine based on their preaching.

Miracles play a role in Luke's theology but a less central role than they play in the other three Gospels. Miracles become events in salvation history; they become signs of the fact that God is acting among people. They provide evidence for faith more than they do in the theology of Mark or Matthew (see Luke 5:1-11; Acts 3:9 ff.).

Sometimes miracle stories provide a model for the ongoing church; the miracles of the apostles are told in terms rather like the terms used for the miracles of Jesus. As we shall see, the same power by which he works miracles is given to them as well.

Some miracle stories in Luke[14]

Luke 5:1-11. The call of the disciples. In Mark's Gospel (1:16-20) Simon and the sons of Zebedee are called to discipleship on the basis of Jesus' word alone. In Luke the call follows the evidence of Jesus' special power in the miracle of the catch of fish. This may originally have been the story of a resurrection appearance (as another version of the same story is in John 21), but here it is clearly the miracle and not the (risen) Lord who evokes Peter's awe (5:8).

The miracles are the signs of God's activity in history, and in response to those signs the men are called to discipleship.

Luke 10:9. The relationship of evidence to faith in Luke is even more clear when we contrast the way he and Matthew treat basically the same material. In Matthew, Jesus says to the disciples:

> "And preach as you go, saying, 'The kingdom of heaven is at hand.' Heal the sick, raise the dead, cleanse lepers, cast out demons . . ." (Matthew 10:7-8).

In Luke Jesus says to the seventy: "Heal the sick . . . and [then] say to them: 'The kingdom of God has come near to you.'"

For Luke the healings are clearly the evidence on which the proclamation of the kingdom is based, the indications that God is at work in history. Of course both Matthew and Luke here suggest that Jesus' miraculous healings provide a model for the disciples and the early church. Luke spells that out when in Acts 3 Peter heals a man and then on the basis of the healing goes on to present a sermon on God's activity in history to the onlookers.

Luke 7:11-23. The widow's son at Nain and John's question to Jesus. In the response of the crowd to Jesus' miraculous raising of the widow's son, we get a good clue to the way in which Luke sees Jesus' miraculous activity to be part of God's saving history. We see the continuity between God's activity under the old covenant and his activity under the new:

> Fear seized them all; and they glorified God, saying, "A great prophet has arisen among us!" and "God has visited his people!" (7:16).

We again see Luke's use of miracles as evidence of God's gracious activity in Jesus' ministry when John's question about Jesus' mission comes in response to the report of the raising at Nain. In Matthew, John's question is in response to Jesus' unspecified "deeds" and follows a section of discourse.

Furthermore while both Matthew and Luke have Jesus point to his healing activity as a sign of his special status when he responds to John, Luke interrupts the dialogue to have Jesus perform a series of miracles on the spot, again providing evidence for his answer: "Go and tell John what you have seen and heard . . ." (7:21-22).

The word "power" (dynamis) in Luke–Acts. Several times in his Gospel, Luke adds a reference to Jesus' "power" to the stories he finds in his sources. In 5:17 he augments Mark 2:2 by saying: "And the power of the Lord was with [Jesus] to heal." Mark has the crowd refer to Jesus' authority, Luke has them refer to his, "authority and power" (4:36). In Luke 6:19, in a summary of Jesus' healings, Luke adds to the reference to the crowd's seeking to touch Jesus: "For power came forth from him and healed them all."

The word "power" in Greek is also a word for "miracle," and the stress on Jesus' miraculous power becomes a link between him and the apostles in Acts (and presumably between Jesus and the later church). The apostles also perform miracles on the basis of the power which has been given them. In Acts 4:7 and 10 Peter's questioners want to know by what *power* he has healed the lame man, and he answers that it is in the name of Jesus of Nazareth that he has done the miracle. In 4:33 it is by great "power" that the apostles testify to Christ's resurrection. Thus, Jesus receives power from God to work miracles and testify to the kingdom; in Jesus' name the apostles receive power to work miracles and testify to Jesus.

Preaching on miracles in Luke

1. Luke's Gospel and Acts are concerned throughout with God's activity in history. The miracle stories can be preached as pointers to the fact that God continues to act in human history as he acted in the history of Jesus and of the early church. They may also become the signs of the kind of freeing, healing activity which properly belongs to God. The miracles become signs of hope in a time when the kingdom seems far away or long delayed. There may be less stress on radical decision in Luke than in Mark or Matthew, but there is a call to patient confidence that God is working out his will in history and particularly in the history of the church.

2. The relationship of faith to miracle is quite different in Luke than it is in Matthew. In Matthew, faith is usually a prerequisite for miracle; in Luke, faith is usually a response to miracle. Onlookers see a miracle and faith begins to grow in them. Usually full faith requires a further word of interpretation (as in Jesus' response to John or Peter's to those who see the lame man healed), but for Luke miracles evoke faith while for Matthew faith evokes miracles. Probably most of us know instances where God's gracious activity evokes faith and other instances where it seems that faith is required to recognize or evince God's gracious activity. Both

emphases therefore can be valuable to our preaching ministry.

3. Finally, the relationship between Christ's miraculous power and the miraculous possibilities for the disciples is clearest in Luke-Acts. Jesus' ministry of healing and liberating love becomes a program for the apostles and presumably for us as well. Whether we can do miracles as spectacular as those in Luke and Acts may seem highly doubtful, but we are called to find the ways in which we can provide healing for those who hurt and proclaim good news to the poor and liberty to the captive. Luke's Gospel assures us that we can and must serve God's saving activity in history.

Miracles in the Gospel of John

Some scholars (notably R. Bultmann) have held that behind John's Gospel there is a "signs" source which contained the basic miracle stories of the first eleven chapters of John. Whether that is the case or not, John has so thoroughly incorporated the signs stories into the rest of his Gospel that we can look at the miracles or signs in the context of his larger theological concerns.

John's theology

In John's Gospel, Jesus is the Revealer who has come from heaven for the purpose of revealing the Father and then returns to heaven to be with the Father (although sometimes it seems as though the living Lord continues to dwell in the believer as well). What Jesus reveals is precisely that he is the Revealer, that in him we see the fullness of who God is. He is the one way to the Father.

Jesus confronts people with judgment, or crisis (the Greek word *krisis* means both). Everyone is forced to choose either for him or against him. To choose for him, to believe that he really is the full revealer of God is to choose light; to choose against him is to choose darkness. Judgment is not some far-off event at the end of time; judgment occurs whenever anyone confronts Jesus.

What Jesus offers is eternal life; that means life after death, presumably, but more than that it means real life in the world, life which is enriched by commitment, by faith, and by love. Those who do not choose life perish. This presumably means that they do not live beyond their physical deaths. It certainly means that they are dead in the midst of life. They refuse the courageous commitment which faithfulness requires, and which alone can make life rich and full.

In John's Gospel, Jesus' crucifixion is not in any sense a defeat; it is a victory. Jesus goes toward the cross with full knowledge of what he is doing, and his last cry is not the cry of abandonment, but the cry of victory: "It is accomplished!"

Crucifixion is a victory because it accomplishes Jesus' return to the Father. Jesus is literally lifted up toward heaven, and that is the first step in his return journey. When he is lifted up, Jesus is able to reveal his glory and to draw all people to himself. When confronted with the crucified Lord, everyone must choose whether to believe or to disbelieve.

The resurrection does not accomplish anything new in John's Gospel; it serves a teaching function. Jesus returns from the tomb before returning to the Father just long enough to comfort the disciples and to explain to them the meaning of his ministry and crucifixion. Then he returns to the Father as he always intended, leaving the Paraclete or Comforter to take his place or, sometimes, to supplement his presence (see John 14:23, 25-29; 16:7-11).

There is an odd tension in John's Gospel between the claim that "the Word became flesh" (which Bultmann takes to be the heart of John's theology) and the claim that "we beheld his glory" (which Ernst Käsemann takes to be the heart of John's theology).[15] Certainly Bultmann is right that the Revealer relates himself to tangible, material realities like bread and water, dies a real death on the cross, and rises with real wounds in his hands and side. The Word does become flesh. However, Käsemann is also right in saying that there is a transparence to the Johannine Jesus which is in striking contrast to the sheer physicality of Mark's Jesus, for example. The Word shines through Jesus so thoroughly that sometimes the flesh is almost invisible; the cross seems too triumphant to be quite human. Jesus always points beyond himself.

Within this theological framework, miracles serve a very important function.[16] In John's Gospel miracles are called either "works" or "signs." From God's side, miracles are works. Works are the deeds which God has been performing throughout history, from creation through the deeds of Moses up to Jesus' own time. They are the concrete ways in which God takes part in human history. At one point, indeed, Jesus refers to his whole ministry as a work (17:4).

From the human side, miracles are signs; they are pointers to

Jesus as the Revealer: the one who reveals the fullness of who God is. The signs are rather like prophetic sign-acts in the Old Testament. They happen not just for their own sake, but they point beyond themselves to God's larger purposes. In John's Gospel signs point to God's larger purposes in Jesus Christ.

Because they are signs, and not just amazing events, miracles are almost always explicitly interpreted in John's Gospel, usually by Jesus himself. Their importance is spelled out for the audience and for the reader. The signs can serve as the *krisis*, the point of judgment where people must choose for Jesus or against him.

Several possible responses to signs are presented in the Gospel. Sometimes Jesus rejects the demand for a sign. When Jesus' opponents demand signs like the Old Testament signs which legitimized Moses, Jesus rejects their demand. True signs need to point to his own person as the Revealer; he need not give the sign of manna, because he is the bread of life (6:30-35).

Sometimes someone sees a sign and fails to believe at all that Jesus is the Revealer. So in the story of the man born blind, even when they acknowledge the reality of the healing, the Jews can only say: "Give God the praise; we know that [Jesus] is a sinner" (9:24).

Sometimes someone sees the signs and believes in them, but does not believe that Jesus really is the full revealer of God. Nicodemus comes to Jesus on the basis of his signs and acknowledges only that Jesus is a teacher sent from God (3:2). Nicodemus's faith is inadequate because it fails to look beyond the signs to Jesus' unique status as the one true revealer of God.

Far better, sometimes someone sees a sign and does believe in Jesus as the revealer of God (2:11). In John 20 Thomas sees the sign of the risen Lord, wounds and all, and at last believes.

Best of all, as Thomas's story makes clear, is to believe that Jesus is the Revealer *without* needing to rely on visible signs:

> Jesus said to him "Have you believed because you have seen me? Blessed are those who have not seen and yet believe" (20:29).

Thus Jesus' (and John's) blessing is reserved for those like the reader who believe on the testimony of the gospel without having seen any signs at all.

Some miracle stories in John

John 2:1-11. The wedding feast at Cana. The story itself is a charming indication of Jesus' gracious activity at an occasion of celebration. More than that, it stands as an example of the contrast between Jesus as the Revealer and the old revelation under the law. (As the prologue has it, "The law was given through Moses; grace and truth came through Jesus Christ," 1:17.)

The new wine which Jesus brings is contrasted to the old water of purification for the Jewish rites. The wine is related to Jesus' "hour [which] has not yet come" (2:4). In John the "hour" is the hour of Jesus' glorification at his crucifixion, and therefore the sign points ahead to the mercy which will be made available in that great event.

There may be hints that the great messianic banquet, a pervasive image in the Gospels and in Jewish sources, has now begun. Certainly there is a kind of nascent Christian faith in the steward's confession: "You have kept the good wine until now" (2:10).

Jesus Christ offers new life over against the old life of Jewish ritual and practice. It is in responding to the sign of that new life, that manifestation of Jesus' "glory," that the disciples first come to faith. This story is therefore a picture of the crisis facing every individual who is asked to choose between the old way of the synagogue and the new way in Jesus. (As the story of the wedding feast points ahead to Jesus' crucifixion, so the next story, relating to the "sign" of the temple's cleansing, points ahead to Jesus' resurrection. Jesus looks beyond the destruction of the Jewish temples to the destruction of the temple of his body and its resurrection in three days [John 2:19]. John makes clear some of his main themes right from the start.)

John 5:1-19. The healing at Bethzatha. Here we see a stress on faith when Jesus asks the man whether he *wants* to be healed (v. 6).

Jesus' opponents insist that even God must obey the law and rest on the sabbath. Jesus insists that God's free grace is not bound by law or traditional expectations, that God is at work even on the sabbath (5:17).

In this passage, Jesus explicitly identifies his miracles as *works.* They are extensions of the works of God and cannot be bound by human customs, like sabbath-keeping (5:17). By identifying his work with God's, Jesus implicitly identified himself with God, and it is this "blasphemy" which continually provokes the division between believers and unbelievers in John's Gospel (vv. 18-19). Again, of course, the miracle is not told for its own sake but is followed by a theological interpretation of what happened.

John 6. The feeding of the multitude. The feeding provides a sign, but the observers misinterpret its meaning, and Jesus has to provide the correct interpretation.

The observers think that the feeding indicates that Jesus fulfills the Jewish expectation of a political messiah, and they seek to make him king. Jesus does not want to be king and therefore makes his escape (6:15). Then in 6:30 the onlookers demand a sign which will be as impressive as the sign Moses performed in the wilderness when he provided manna for the children of Israel. Jesus insists that it is not his job to provide a sign, but that he himself *is* the sign. He is the one who points to God; he is the one who gives real and lasting life. It is not that he gives manna; he *is* true manna. It is in relation to him that people can find eternal life (6:35, 51).

In this passage the complex attitude of John's Gospel toward signs becomes most clear. Signs are ambiguous. Signs can be misinterpreted to suggest that Jesus is a prophet or a king in the line of Jewish prophets and kings, or signs can be correctly interpreted to point to Jesus as the true Revealer. Even then, what the signs reveal is that Jesus himself is the *real* sign. He is the one true pointer to the reality of God the Father.

John 9. The man born blind. Here the stress on judgment and crisis comes clearest of all. "Jesus said, 'For judgment I came into this world, that those who do not see may see, and that those who see may become blind'" (9:39).

Judgment is clearly not a future but a present phenomenon. Judgment takes place precisely as people respond to Christ. Those who confess him see; those who deny him (though they think they see) are blind.

A miracle, a sign, the healing of the man born blind, becomes the occasion of *krisis*, of judgment. The sign occasions faith in the man born blind. (He shows no faith in Jesus prior to the healing; he does not even ask to see, 9:6-7.) The sign occasions unfaith in the Pharisees. Again they think that God's activity must be bound to old ways and old expectations. Healing on the sabbath is ruled out (9:24). God has spoken only to Moses (9:29). The man born blind pays dearly for his faithfulness: he is excommunicated (9:34). The Pharisees pay far more dearly: they are condemned to blindness and to enduring sin (9:41).

John 11. Lazarus. We shall have occasion to discuss this story at greater length in chapter 5 when we talk about resurrection in John. We can here note a few features which are appropriate to our discussion of miracles.

Once again the sign of the raising of Lazarus becomes an occasion for Jesus to elucidate right theology, to make clear the meaning of his mission. Martha provides a foil for Jesus. She never does quite understand, but she provides Jesus the opportunity to explain what his life-giving mission really means.

Once again the miracle becomes a *krisis*, the occasion for judgment. On the one hand, many of the Jews see what Jesus has done and believe in him. On the other hand, some go and incite the Pharisees to kill Jesus. Interestingly, in John's Gospel the raising of Lazarus is the event which is responsible for the furious opposition to Jesus. It is Jesus' life-giving power which is a fundamental threat to the old traditions which his opponents seek to defend.

Finally we have here the phrase "I am the resurrection and the life." The phrase "I am" *(ego eimi)* occurs time and again in John's Gospel (for instance in "*I am* the bread of life," 6:35). In the Greek Bible *ego eimi* were the first words of God's response in Exodus 3:14 to Moses when Moses asked his name. Whenever Jesus uses this phrase in John's Gospel, he is really identifying himself with Yahweh, the Lord of Israel. In so doing, Jesus either commits terrible blasphemy or makes an audacious and life-giving claim.

Preaching on miracles in John

Again we can only suggest some central themes.

1. The miracles in John's Gospel are invariably presented as part of a dramatic dialogue. The drama is central to the story which is being told. Positions are taken, sides drawn, options suggested. Almost always our preaching from John's miracle stories should take advantage of their highly dramatic character. We can see the scenes as scenes, the characters as characters. We lose some of their richness by trying to reduce them to didactic treatises.

2. John's Gospel, more clearly than the other Gospels, indicates that miracles are not told for their own sake; they always point beyond themselves to a deeper theological meaning. Because the deeper theological meaning is usually spelled out, it is sometimes easier to preach on the *meaning* of a miracle story in John than it is in the Synoptics (and more immediately acceptable to our congregations).

3. Finally, for John there is really only one sign, and that is Jesus himself, the full revealer of God. The other signs are only derivative; they are signs because they point to him and he points to God. For in John's Gospel the incarnation of Jesus validates the signs, rather than the signs proving the incarnation. Right Christian preaching needs always to take account of the fact that we proclaim Christ first; we proclaim miracles only in relation to the central miracle of his grace.

4. John's Gospel, more clearly than the others, calls the reader or listener to a kind of decision. With almost frightening clarity, we are presented with a choice: life or death, light or darkness, belief or unbelief. More than any other Gospel, John confronts the preacher and the congregation with decision—not decision for or against the truth of a miracle story, of course, but decision for or against the truth and grace which are in Jesus Christ.

CHAPTER 3

Demons,
the Demonic,
Exorcism

In recent years there has been a remarkable revival of interest in demons and demonic possession within Western society. While theologians have been willing enough to talk about the "demonic," the question of the reality of demons has largely been ignored as hopelessly old-fashioned or beside the point. Outside the realm of scholarly theology, however, there has been a conspicuous growth of popular interest in demons. Magazines devoted to demons, witches, and the occult are sold at drug stores and supermarkets. Occult bookstores flourish in a number of our urban centers. TV plays deal soberly if not seriously with tales of haunted houses and possessed children; and *The Exorcist*, a remarkably popular book, has been made into an incredibly popular motion picture.

This new interest in demons has affected the main line churches as well. In England an Anglican priest has built his reputation largely on his purported capacity to perform exorcisms. In the United States pastors, somewhat embarrassed, swap stories of troubled parishioners who come to them asking to be rid of demons. Among "liberals" and "evangelicals" alike, forums and seminars on demons and exorcisms draw large and curious crowds.

Demons and Exorcism in the New Testament

We leave it to sociologists, psychologists, and historians of religion to explain the sudden revival. Our hope in this chapter is to give some background from the New Testament on the nature of demons in a biblical context, and some hints from a pastoral perspective on the ways in which main line churches may respond helpfully to the renewed interest in the demonic and in demons. Then we hope to suggest some ways in which the idea of the "demonic" and of "exorcism" may be useful to the church's pastoral and social ministries in our time.

"Demons" in New Testament times

In the time between the Old and New Testaments, Jewish writings largely explained the origin of demons on the basis of an obscure text in Genesis 6:

> When men began to multiply on the face of the ground, and daughters were born to them, the sons of God saw that the daughters of men were fair; and they took to wife such of them as they chose. Then the Lord said, "My spirit shall not abide in man for ever, for he is flesh, but his days shall be a hundred and twenty years." The Nephilim [giants] were on the earth in those days, and also afterward, when the sons of God came in to the daughters of men, and they bore children to them (6:1-4a).

Apparently these "giants" were held responsible for the evil on the earth (described in Genesis 6:5), and when they died their spirits remained to haunt the earth as demons. (See, for example, I Enoch 15:8 ff.; Jubilees 4:22; 5:1-9.)

In the rabbinic literature (whose precise dating is very difficult to ascertain), one rabbi suggests that the demons were begotten by Adam in the years before he was 130, because it was only after that time that he begot sons in his own image, as Genesis 5:3 makes clear.[1] Elsewhere, certain rabbis held that the demons were created by God late on the Friday of creation and left unfinished because the sabbath fell before God had time to fashion their bodies.[2]

Sometimes the demons have a chief—variously called Beliar, Belial, Mastema, or Satan.[3]

Intertestamental writings hold that demons are responsible for a variety of ills. "And the spirits of the giants afflict, oppress, destroy, attack, do battle, and work destruction on the earth, and cause trouble" (I Enoch 15:11).

Two factors help to account for the rise in the belief in demons during the period just before Jesus. One factor was the growing concern with the "problem of evil." God's promises to his people Israel seemed to have been shattered. First came the exile and then the return, utterly devoid of the glory and promise the great prophets had predicted. The faithful were faced with oppression from without and treason from within. When the faithful remnant arose under the Maccabees their victory was short-lived. Some of the Maccabee heroes perished; others sold out to their Hellenizing enemies. It seemed impossible that a good God could be responsible for these disasters, so increasingly the responsibility for the way the world went was shifted to demonic, evil forces.

Furthermore, in an increasingly syncretistic society, the dualistic religions of Persia, with their stress on the struggle between good and evil forces, came increasingly to influence Jewish thought. The idols and false gods of the Old Testament came to be identified with demonic forces and the world was increasingly perceived as a battleground between the forces of God and the forces of Satan.

Of course it was not just this historical and religious change in Israel which accounted for the belief in demons. The belief in demons was used to explain real, observed phenomena.

Both Jewish and non-Jewish sources ascribe a variety of ills, distresses, and odd behavior to demonic possession and their cure to exorcism. Even Lucian, who is skeptical of the stories he tells, describes the symptoms of people purported to be possessed ". . . everyone knows about the Syrian from Palestine, the adept in it, how many he takes in hand who fall down in the light of the moon and roll their eyes and fill their mouths with foam. . . ."[4]

And however one explains the symptoms of the exorcism stories in Mark 5:1-20 or Mark 9:14-29, there can be no doubt that real phenomena are being described.

Therefore, for a good many Jews in the time leading up to Jesus' ministry, the world was perceived as a battleground between good and evil spiritual forces, between the forces of God and the forces of the demons.

Jesus and the demons

Into this world divided between good and evil forces came Jesus, the preacher and exorcist. One of the great hopes of the Jewish people was that God's final rule, his kingdom, would soon

come, and one sign of that kingdom would be the overcoming of
the powers of evil, the demons. So we find in one of the
"intertestamental" writings:

> Then the Mighty One of Israel shall glorify Shem,
> For the Lord God shall appear on earth,
> And Himself save men.
> Then shall all the spirits of deceit be given
>   to be trodden under foot,
> And men shall rule over wicked spirits.
>   (Testament of Simeon, 6:5-6)[5]

Jesus clearly saw his own ministry as a decisive battle in the war
to establish the kingdom of God over the kingdom of the demons.
It was not just that his defeat of evil spirits was a sign or symbol of
the kingdom; his defeat of evil spirits was a victory for the
kingdom. Every time demons were overthrown, Jesus won
another skirmish for the kingdom of God. So in one of the
indisputably authentic sayings of Jesus, he says: "But if it is by the
finger [Spirit] of God that I cast out demons, then the kingdom of
God has come upon you" (Luke 11:20; Matthew 12:28).

It must be added that Jesus does not claim to be unique in his
power to cast out demons. In Luke 11:19 he says to his Jewish
opponents, "If I cast out demons by Beelzebul, by whom do your
sons cast them out?" The obvious assumption is that the Jewish
exorcists are also casting out demons; and when Jesus goes on to
speak about the in-breaking of the kingdom of God, the implication is that the Jewish exorcisms are also signs of that kingdom.

The New Testament (and Jesus himself) therefore *assumes* the
reality of demons, and before we look at the reality of demons and
the meaning of the demonic in our own time, we need to look at the
marks of the demonic and of exorcism in the ministry of Jesus.

The Nature of Demons and Exorcism in the Ministry of Jesus

As our evidence for the nature of the demonic and of exorcism in
Jesus' time, we use the exorcism stories as they were found in the
pre-Markan source and particularly that story which lies behind
Mark 5:1-20.

There are five marks which distinguish the demonic in the early
exorcism stories about Jesus.

1. The demonic is beyond human control and beyond the
control of the person who is possessed. This is perhaps most

evident in the description of the demoniac in Mark 5:3-4: "[The man] lived among the tombs; and no one could bind him any more, even with a chain . . . no one had the strength to subdue him." In this story and elsewhere when Jesus addresses the possessed, he always addresses the demons, not the demoniac. He recognizes that those who are possessed are not really in control of themselves.

2. The demonic is not merely outside human control, it is hurtful. It inflicts injury on the one possessed. This is again most evident in the story in Mark 5:5: "Night and day among the tombs and on the mountains he was always crying out, and bruising himself with stones." The reminder that the demonic is harmful is present as well in Mark 9:22, where the father speaks of the demon's treatment of his son: "And it has often cast him into the fire and into the water, to destroy him. . . ."

3. The demonic is isolating; it separates the possessed from community and even from healing. In each of the exorcism stories, the demon tries to protect the isolation of the possessed by telling Jesus to go away. Again in the story in Mark 5 the isolation of the demoniac is particularly clear; the man lives among the tombs, totally separated from home and companionship, resisting all attempts at human or divine help.

4. The demonic aspires to absolute power. The words of the demons in Mark 1:24 and 5:7 are formulas by which these lesser powers try to overcome the absolute power of God in Jesus Christ. They are not satisfied with being minor dignitaries in the company of the divine, but with overweening pride they try to out-maneuver the absolute authority of Jesus.

5. The demonic, unlike the conventional evil represented by the Pharisees, can actually recognize the reality of Jesus' holiness. The demonic is clear on the nature and power of the enemy, and therefore the demonic actually discerns the kingdom. (See again Mark 1:24; 5:7; 9:20.)

There are also six marks of exorcism in these stories, six signs of the healing which is necessary to overcome the demonic powers.

1. In exorcism the salvation from the demonic always comes from outside the possessed. The demoniac is not able to overcome the powers which threaten his own well-being. In this sense Tillich is right in saying that the "changing power" in overcoming the demonic split in men and society must be a "divine structure, that is, a structure of grace."[6]

2. The exorcist recognizes the demonic for what it is. Jesus does not attempt to overcome the powers of the demonic by dealing with the possessed, but by dealing first of all with the demonic powers. He does not say to the demoniac, "Buck up!" or "Have faith!" He says to the demons, "Come out of him!" (Mark 1:25).

3. In exorcism healing always takes place at the point of most resistance. It is when the demonic powers in the demoniac cry out most angrily against Jesus that healing can take place.

4. The exorcisms involve a power struggle. In the New Testament understanding of power, of course, this is the struggle between powerful words or between supernatural forces which recognize one another. They yell devastating words at one another in a battle of life and death.

5. The power of the exorcist is exercised by means of a word rather than by any concrete physical action. In the biblical milieu, words have a power which is scarcely comprehensible to us today, and that power is evident in the fact that Jesus' words effect the exorcism; there is nothing more to be done.

6. In the exorcism stories the mark of healing is that the one who had been possessed lives in calm instead of frenzy and in community instead of isolation. This is again especially evident in the story of the demoniac of the tombs, where the healed man, who had been frantically running about and hurting himself, is found "clothed and in his right mind" (Mark 5:15). At the end of the story, when the demoniac wants to stay with Jesus to protect his isolation by allegiance to a new supernatural power, Jesus insists rather that he is to "go home to [his] friends . . ." (5:19).

Demons and Exorcism in the Ministry of the Church Today

I pretend to no expertise in either pastoral ministry or in the community ministry of the church; I bring only my brief and uncertain experience as a pastor to the analysis of the demonic and exorcism in the church's ministry. Yet the biblical picture of the demonic and of exorcism does seem to me helpful for understanding some aspects of our ministry today. (We shall speak in the concluding section of this chapter on the "reality" of demons.)

The demonic and exorcism in the church's pastoral ministry

The marks of the demonic provide useful clues for recognizing *one* kind of need to which pastoral ministry should respond. The demonic is not, of course, descriptive of every kind of problem which is faced by pastors.

1. When someone perceives himself to be under the control of outside forces, that is one hint that we may diagnose his condition as "demonic." People suffering from some kinds of mental illness perceive themselves to be under outside control, but more prosaic instances may also have touches of the demonic. Many who have counseled people suffering from drug addiction or alcoholism or a kind of antisocial and undifferentiated lust will realize that those people often seem to be more controlled than controlling, victims rather than agents. To this extent they are "possessed" by forces which are demonic.

2. A second hint that a person may be under the power of the "demonic" is that the person consistently and unwillingly hurts himself. The demoniac is his own worst enemy. The injury inflicted is usually not as dramatic as striking oneself with stones, but it may consist of suicidal drinking bouts, devastating doses of drugs, unthinking lust which destroys the very relationships the possessed most cherishes.

3. The third hint that a person is "possessed" is that he isolates himself or is isolated from family, friends, and community. The desperate drive toward secrecy (which is, of course, a subtle form of isolation) is a clue to the presence of the demonic. The secret fix, the secret drink, the secret appointment at the anonymous motel are all devices by which the demonic serves to isolate the demoniac. The lies, the creeping incredulity among family and friends, the deadening of trust—all intensify the desperate isolation of the demoniac. The demoniac wards off attempts at help because he will not admit his need for help.

4. Further, when the very forces which threaten to destroy the personality are somehow justified as being especially good, especially holy, especially worthy of preserving, when they aspire not to relative power but to absolute power, we can suspect that the forces are most demonic: "I drink a lot and I'm proud of it." "I really tripped out last week!" "I met the greatest woman in Chicago last weekend." We have heard (or used) those lines. They are the desperate attempts at rationalization, at self-justification, which can mark the demonic. (All of us have seen in ourselves and others the odd, paradoxical shift between secrecy and boasting;

between hiding our habits and flaunting them before others.)

5. Finally, when the person who is "possessed" by these debilitating forces shows great fear and resistance to any word of help or healing, toward any attempt to overcome the false isolation or the false self-justification of the demonic, we can again suggest that the pained person is experiencing something analogous to possession described in the New Testament. The very recognition of the power and threat of the divine enemy shows the demonic for what it is.

The six marks of exorcism in Jesus' ministry may also provide help for the church in dealing with those who seem to be "possessed." Again we can hardly provide a complete prescription for dealing with possession. All we can do is provide some clues from the New Testament stories which may be of use in our pastoral ministry today.

1. In exorcism the salvation from the demonic always comes from outside the possessed. Therefore as the gospel proclaims from first to last, the word of healing can never be: "Save yourself," or in contemporary language, "Buck up!" or "Snap out of it!" Healing can come only as a gift. For the Christian the gift of exorcism comes in Jesus Christ, and the right words of exorcism (however demythologized or reinterpreted) can only be: "I charge you *in the name of Jesus Christ* to come out!" (Acts 16:18).

2. Exorcism requires the recognition that the demonic forces are outside the victim's control. Questions of blame or responsibility— however helpful in some pastoral care situations—are hardly useful in dealing with the person distressed by demonic forces. However antisocial or unpleasant the possessed person may seem, he is first of all a victim, and the struggle is to be fought, not against him, but against the forces which drive him.

3. Since exorcism takes place at the point of most resistance, the Christian as exorcist will try to be aware of the phenomenon of resistance and will be ready to recognize in resistance precisely the sign that healing is possible. The points at which the demoniac is most threatened by the possibility of healing are often the points at which healing can most readily take place.[7]

4. Exorcism involves a power struggle. The Christian exorcist will necessarily be involved in the expenditure of time and energy, in the exhausting involvement which sticks by the demoniac and refuses to let go until the demon is exorcised. This, of course, in no

way denies the necessity for the pastor or church counselor or concerned Christian to refer cases of clinical disease to competent psychologists or physicians. We rather suggest that even in cases of more standard pastoral care, the intensive feeling with and for the patient bears all the marks of a power struggle; it is intensive and exhausting.

5. Exorcism is performed by a word. The content of the word, of course, will differ from instance to instance, and usually it will not be a single word but an ongoing expression of feeling and concern between pastor and parishioner, between friend and friend. The story of the demoniac of the tombs suggests that the healing word will be one which refuses to accept the demoniac's isolation. The healing word is a word which refuses to let go, and the presence of the exorcist with and for the demoniac is itself a means toward salvation.

As Acts 16:18 indicates, the word which is pronounced against the demonic forces is a word which is pronounced in the name of Jesus Christ. In that sense, right preaching can itself be exorcism. Where Christ is preached as the one who overcomes demonic forces, Christ is present as the one who overcomes demonic forces. Sometimes, perhaps, the word of healing will come with sudden and astonishing power. More often the preacher tries continually and faithfully to proclaim the word of healing, hoping and believing that slowly God is winning his victory over the devious forces of evil which thwart and possess us all.

6. The marks of healing, the results of exorcism correctly performed, as we would expect, are serenity and love: the ability to live with oneself without anxiety and with others in affection and mutual concern. Wherever one can come to accept oneself and to love others, there is a victory for the kingdom, and the powers of darkness suffer another defeat.

The demonic and exorcism in the church's social ministry

The marks of what can be called "demonic" are also evident in the structures of American society in our day, and the marks of exorcism can provide useful clues for the church as it undertakes a ministry of healing within that society.

We look first at the marks of the "demonic" in American society.

1. The demonic forces are beyond human, or at least individual, control. Surely there is some reality behind the contemporary

mythological language: "the Establishment," "the Military-Industrial Complex." As with any mythological language, the element of truth is veiled and somewhat distorted, but it points to the reality of a society in which structures and institutions have often gone beyond the control of persons, where all of us are to some extent victims of the institutions we have created and thought we controlled.

On the other hand, there is the sense in which those who protest against the oppressiveness of contemporary institutions can become victims of their ideology. The Movement can take on a reality of its own, divorced from human needs and aspirations. Its vision gets shaped, not by the empirical grit of the world but by large Principles to which empirical reality is forced to conform.

In both of these cases, the demonic is not to be confused with the possessed. The guardian of the military-industrial establishment and the rebel with a cause are both in part victims of realities which they did not create and which threaten the fullness of their own humanity. In analyzing the demonic, it is necessary to distinguish between the subservient evil of those who participate in the demonic and the controlling evil of those demonic forces which possess them.

There is a strong and right tendency in Christianity to locate evil within the individual, but the exorcism stories provide a necessary reminder that sometimes we do battle with forces larger and more frightening than the particular sins of any individual:

> For we are not contending against flesh and blood, but against the principalities, against the powers, against the world rulers of this present darkness, against the spiritual hosts of wickedness in the heavenly places (Ephesians 6:12).

2. The demonic forces are not only superhuman, they are antihuman, or, in the current jargon, dehumanizing. Certainly in American society all the structures of the oppressor conspire against the humanity of the oppressed, whether deliberately or unintentionally. The literature of various minorities (and of the women's movement) in America in recent years has made clear how a whole societal structure can be profoundly dehumanizing.

From the other side, however, hatred is also dehumanizing. It dehumanizes both the hater and the hated: the hater because he pretends to be more than human and to stand in judgment over another; the hated because he is demeaned to something less than human.

Hatred represents the fundamental failure to distinguish between the demoniac and the demons. It is itself demonic. When any one of us confuses the subservient evil in which we all share with that controlling evil which transcends us, he himself falls victim to a confusion which is fundamentally antihuman and therefore demonic.

Group pride has played a necessary role in the struggle of oppressed minorities to overcome oppression. Prudentially and even humanistically it is perhaps wrong for the affluent, established, and secure Christian to remind his oppressed brothers and sisters that hatred is demonic and in its own way as dehumanizing as oppression. But the Christian mode can never be first of all prudential or humanistic; it must first of all be faithful. In the economy of faith there is no place for hatred. The church as exorcist says a fundamental "No" to hatred, however justified it may be from psychological, sociological, or political points of view.

3. The demonic forces are isolating. The demonic background of the present social structure in America is nowhere more evident than in the extent to which we are isolated from one another.

This isolation is predominantly and shamefully evident in the whole reality of a ghetto society, where we who are affluent, white, and comfortable have forced the poor, the nonwhite, and the disadvantaged into islands within our communities. Then we have barricaded ourselves behind makeshift fortresses and prayed that no one will break down the dividing wall of hostility.

Yet here, presumptuously again perhaps, we can only add that the understanding of minority pride, which means minority isolation, has to be denied by the Christian. The kingdom of God is the kingdom which moves toward the community of all persons under God. Any movement which works against community and toward isolation, from whatever motives, is therefore to be rejected.

And what shall we say for the segregated church? How can it be that at this late date we need even stop to raise the question whether the church has any right to be a sign of human isolation rather than a sign of human community? Every church which is deliberately segregated, whatever other grace may there abound, lives under the sign of the demonic powers. And every church which is segregated because of the circumstances of its location, its affluence, its theology, its sophistication, its history, must at least raise the question of whether the kingdom does not demand that location, affluence, theology, sophistication, and history not be used as banners under which the demons of isolation can march.

4. The demonic pretends to absolute divinity. We can suspect that patriotism has become demonic precisely when it becomes idolatrous, when it demands, not simply what belongs to Caesar, but what belongs to God as well. The American "civil religion" becomes demonic precisely when it becomes a religion, when it demands, not relative allegiance, but total loyalty.

We can see the demonic at work in a corporate society when corporations hire their own evangelists and no longer sell simply a product but a way of life, a mode of salvation—giving us cars in which we are supposed to believe, friends at a bank, and love in a carbonated drink.

Then, of course, we must also say that the Movement which resists the enticements of the American corporate state sometimes tries to take on the attributes of God as well. Revolution becomes an absolute reality to be apprehended only by a pure leap of faith. The advocates of revolution take on the aura of the saints and prophets. The very secularization of the word *charisma* points to a situation where spirit is confused with *the* Spirit and genuine heroes are turned into fake gods.

5. Perhaps the most elusive quality of the demonic, yet one which is particularly suggestive, is the ability of the demonic to recognize Jesus for who he is (and, as in Acts 16:17, to recognize the power of those who fight with Jesus against the demonic).

In the Gospels the Jewish leaders represent one kind of opposition to Jesus. They simply refuse or are unable to under-stand who Jesus is and therefore try to get rid of him as a genuine nuisance.

The demonic's opposition to Jesus is quite different from that. The demons know with a terrible clarity who Jesus is, and therefore they try to get rid of him as a fundamental threat. In the demonic response to Jesus there is no calm argument, no clever question; there is only the cry of recognition, fear, and rage.

One can therefore suspect that the demonic is to be seen in the attempts of those who want to silence the church when it speaks out against the status quo. When such forces respond with considerable vigor and power, they show the extent to which the church (from time to time) may represent the genuinely threatening power of the kingdom of God. That is, wherever the establishment loses its temper and threatens to take the church seriously, there the demonic realities come closest to the surface; there the church may indeed more faithfully be representing the kingdom than is its wont.

On the other side, we may say that whenever the counterculture or the oppressed peoples most violently resist the church's word against isolation and for community, then we can suspect that the revolutionaries have been possessed by forces beyond their own control, that they are no longer living according to their own full humanity. We may hope that their anger is a sign that the church has found a way to be faithful to the kingdom of God which is first a kingdom for persons and not a kingdom for causes, however just.

We must finally say that the church itself stands in special danger of being possessed by the demonic. Whenever church structures move beyond human control, whenever the church protects itself to the detriment of human good, whenever the church is isolated or isolating, whenever the church asks to be worshiped instead of worshiping, whenever the church reacts angrily against those Christian or secular prophets who threaten its comfort, we can suspect that something of the demonic has entered into the church's life.

In seeking to do battle against the demonic, the church would do well to pay attention to the beam in its own eye, though it cannot simply ignore the multitude of specks in the eyes of the society around it. The kingdom always stands over against the church while it is also symbolized in the church. The church is both the sign of the kingdom and an enemy of the kingdom. In that sense, the church is like the demoniac of the tombs who, though he does not know it, is about to become a servant of the Christ who threatens him.

The six marks of exorcism in Jesus' ministry provide clues for the church's ministry to the demonic in American society.

1. The fact that exorcism always comes from *outside* the possessed reminds the church that the healing word it speaks must always be a word of grace and judgment. The word must be a word of grace because it is always a gift and not an achievement of

the possessed. It must be a word of judgment because salvation always stands outside any institutional structure or revolutionary program. The fact that the power of exorcism comes from outside the possessed suggests that the claim to saving power on the part of persons or institutions is itself demonic. Healing can only come when social institutions or political movements forgo the claim to have authority equal to that of Jesus.

2. The exorcist recognizes the demonic for what it is. In the same way, the church resists the attempt to identify the reality of evil with specifically evil persons. It resists the efforts to stereotype or to isolate. It is wary of labeling individuals and of demeaning persons. Further, because it recognizes that the demonic (though not all evil) is to be found in those forces which are more than human, the church as exorcist is profoundly concerned with changing structures and institutions. It is not content with attempts to change the human heart, since in contemporary American society, at least, even the good-hearted are often victims of demeaning forces beyond their control.

3. Since healing often takes place at the point of most resistance, where chaos and confusion come to a head, the church in our society must be wary of those who see all social convulsion as necessarily evil and who sue for false peace under false colors. To be sure, hatred, anger, radical social disturbance, fear, and desperate attempts at self-defense are hardly signs of the kingdom. They may show the profound ambivalence of a society caught between the old demonic powers and the new powers of healing. The church has the obligation to stand at the points of convulsion and to try to bring the word of reconciliation, but to stifle the convulsions prematurely might only be to postpone the inevitable and necessary struggle.

4. Since exorcism involves a power struggle, the church will need to be less afraid of using the power it has. To be sure, every use of power carries with it the potential for the demonic, and every absolutizing of power is indeed demonic, but it can safely be said that the problem with the American church today is not an excess of the willingness to use power. The kingdom comes not only in word but in power. In the currency of America, that means power of protest, of organization, and almost certainly economic power—power used to support movements toward community and humanity, power refused to any group whose goal is isolation,

whose motive is hatred, and whose fruit is oppression of others.

5. In exorcism the power is exercised by means of a word rather than by a concrete physical action. This surely means that preaching can and should be one of the powerful means by which the church symbolizes and enacts the kingdom and does battle against the demonic. Perhaps we can go even further and say that, however elliptically, Jesus' exorcisms give us a model for a struggle which is powerful but not physically violent. It may be stretching the point, but the good citizens who thought that the way to heal the demoniac of the tombs was to bind him by physical force found that his force could outdo theirs (Mark 5:4). Healing came when Jesus refused violence without refusing forcefulness. There is no clear directive for the church here. The line between legitimate power and illegitimate violence is hard to draw. Jesus' cleansing of the temple reminds us that he could *act* powerfully. However the exorcisms provide a suggestive picture. Jesus gave a person his freedom but did not coerce him into freedom. One might think that that is the only way freedom comes, for a person or for a society.

6. Finally, the marks of healing were serenity and love. Translated for American society, the marks of healing would be peace and community. False peace without community would not be healing. The ghettoized peace of America in the seventies is a mere truce and not the fullness of healing as we find it in the New Testament stories. The picture of an America in peace and community seems so foreign as to be futile, but it stands over against us as a judgment and a call, as a very dim, imperfect, persuasive parable of what life in society is presumably meant to be. In that sense it is a very dim, imperfect, persuasive parable of the kingdom of God. For the practical, it may look like a lost cause; for the faithful, it looks like the only cause not certain of losing.

We can say one more word about the nature of exorcism in our time. Though it is hard to get at its original form, the story of the strange exorcist in Mark 9:38-40 (and the reference by Jesus to exorcisms performed by Jewish exorcists, in Luke 11:19) suggests that Jesus recognized the work of the kingdom in exorcisms which were not performed by him or by those who were explicitly part of his band. Jesus suggested that those who were not against him were "for him," that is, they were his allies in the great ongoing battle of the kingdom (Mark 9:40).

With his strong statement, Jesus suggests that the battle of the kingdom is not limited to those who explicitly enroll in that battle. In a sense he recognizes an Order of Fellow-Travelers, or a fifth column for the kingdom. Put in contemporary terms, we who are in the church should be neither surprised nor disappointed that there are those outside the church who are doing battle against the demonic. They can serve as a judgment on us, a reminder that the kingdom is greater than the church and that any attempt on our part to confuse the two is itself demonic. They can also serve as a sign of great hope to us, the hope that God's purpose is greater even than his people (or that there are more of his people than we would have expected), that the kingdom is not only among us but around us.

We do not need to go to the fellow-travelers and congratulate them on being crypto-Christians. Presumably they would not be flattered. But secretly we can rejoice at every point where people do battle against the more than human, antihuman forces we call demonic. We can rejoice at every point where human serenity and love, where social peace and community increase. The kingdom is there. Christ is there, whether Christians are there or not.

Are There Any "Real" Demons Today?

Our discussion of the "demonic" leaves unanswered the questions of whether there are any "real" demons, or whether people are sometimes "really" possessed.

The questions are unavoidable. Entertainments like *The Exorcist* and the growth of interest in a great variety of occult phenomena force us to try to look seriously at the question. While I was giving lectures on the demonic at the Graduate Theological Union in Berkeley, students regularly pushed me to speak, not about the demonic but about demons, to respond to strange experiences they had had, to stories of possession they could tell.

More than that, the concept of demons which seems strangely quaint and old-fashioned to Western "rational" Christians is still an important and vital concept among some of the Third World churches. At about the time that I finished my dissertation on exorcism as a problem in New Testament historical and theological studies, a friend from Zaire finished a dissertation on exorcism as a mode of pastoral care, an approach to ministry which was still vital in his own community.

Yet if the question of the reality of demons is unavoidable, our answer can only be evasive. We can try to make a few suggestions which may throw some light on the dark side of Christian theological concern.

First, there is truth in the line from *Hamlet:* "There are more things in heaven and earth, Horatio, than are dreamt of in your philosophy." The interest among young people in the occult and the odd is in part a response to their elders' overzealous attempt to demystify the universe. Just when we think we have the world contained in a Freudian or Marxist or empiricist or Bultmannian cage, some inexplicable oddity sneaks through the bars and plays freely outside, at the edges of our perception. I for one am not very enthusiastic about making demons or ghosts (the issue for Hamlet and Horatio) or parapsychic phenomena the heart of our theology. Nevertheless, those of us who listen very often to the stories people tell late at night when they are not worried about being rational will have to admit that sometimes our careful philosophies cannot contain the rich and odd diversity of what is.

Second, all of us who work in biblical theology, all of us who try to be faithful Christians, need to be nervous about the attempt to reduce images and words from one discipline or one realm of discourse to images and words from another realm of discourse. Grace is not just self-acceptance, though it is related to that. Ancient Israel's status as the Chosen People is not just a matter of the peculiar political and economic organization of the early tribes, though it is related to that organization. The role of the prophets cannot simply be explained in terms of their psychological makeup, nor the Damascus vision as a striking epileptic seizure, whether epilepsy was involved or not. In the same way the people that the New Testament calls "possessed" are *something* like people we could call psychotic or, sometimes, epileptic today, but they are not exactly the same. Exorcism sometimes looks like a (remarkably short) course of psychotherapy, or a paradigm of the dialectic struggle between Spirit and antispirit, but exorcism is not *exactly* that. Stories of possession and exorcism are richer than our attempts to translate them into other language. Statements about demons are richer than our statements about the demonic. There is more there than meets the skeptical eye or fits the rational definition. If the goodness of God and the majesty of his kingdom defy simple definition, so does the evil against which he fights.

Third, in our first chapter we spoke of miracles as events for which there are alternative explanations. It is not necessarily the case that one explanation of a miracle is valid and the other invalid. It is rather that one explanation informs our understanding and elicits our response in one way, another explanation informs our understanding and elicits our response in another way. To explain a particular case of emotional disturbance in terms derived from Freudian psychology may be helpful in our understanding and in our attempts to bring healing. To explain it in terms derived from more classical biblical categories, terms like "possession" may also help our understanding and enrich our capacity to heal. Certainly when we enrich language about therapy or social action with language about exorcism, we shift the focus from human capacities and programs to God's activity in bringing his kingdom. The Christian must say that sometimes that shift enriches our insight and provokes our faithfulness.[8]

Fourth, psychological and social analysis is often based on what we can call *useful constructs*. I have never seen a demon, but then neither have I ever seen an ego, a superego, or an id. I am not sure what it means to talk about a "real" demon, but I am not sure what it means to talk about a "real" market economy or a "real" dialectic. We grab at words and fashion models to help us predict what is apt to happen, which helps us cope with the immense diversity and the rapid change of the environment in which we live. For some people in some circumstances, it may be useful to talk about unconscious realities, about the pressure of the superego on the id. For some people in some circumstances, it may be more useful to talk about "spiritual" realities, about the pressure of demons on the soul. Sometimes historical analysis can proceed most helpfully by looking to Marxist categories, like the struggle of the proletariat against capitalist oppression. Sometimes historical analysis can proceed most helpfully by looking to biblical categories, like the battle of God's kingdom against demonic oppression. We reduce our options for analysis and for helpful action by ruling any model out of court by fiat or by bias. The richest approach to personal healing and to social action will probably be oddly pluralistic, seeing in the rich diversity of explanations and approaches the rich diversity of the universe. (For the Christian, the rich diversity of the creation mirrors the rich diversity of the Creator.)

This, of course, has very practical implications for the pastor who is dealing with cases of emotional and spiritual need. While my own biases tend strongly toward traditional therapeutic methods and a great reliance on professionally trained therapists, and while I would always urge the use of some of these methods as a first resort, there may be times when the most helpful mode of healing is to take seriously the self-perception of the person who wishes to be healed.

If someone comes to us and explains his need in Freudian terms, we need at least to be able to take those terms seriously. If someone comes and starts talking about his Parent threatening his Child, that is not the time for us to launch into a little lecture on the foolishness of Transactional Analysis, whether we believe it to be foolish or not. If someone comes to us and claims to be possessed by demons, we do little good by remarking on the irrationality of that claim. Sometimes, at least as a last resort, in concert with all the other modes of healing we can bring, we need to take that self-perception seriously. We need to be willing to perform actual exorcisms, as best we can. In fear and trembling and reliance on the grace of God we need to use devices we can scarcely begin to understand. Some of the churches have specific rites of exorcism included in their liturgy, and pastors would do well to keep such rites at hand in case we are called upon to use them.

These paragraphs are, of course, an elaborate hedge. They do not answer or even pretend to answer the question of whether demons "exist." They are an attempt to provide some clues for dealing with the increasingly widespread belief in demons.

There is one affirmation which the Christian can make unequivocally, however. That is that God in Christ has conquered and is conquering and will continue to conquer all which demeans humanity and destroys human community. Because that faith is absolute, we need not get too concerned about the relative question of whether or not to believe in demons. If there are any demons, they are shadow players in the drama of God's action, already doomed to be driven foolishly from the stage with no one to mourn their loss. And because that faith is absolute, we can unashamedly try to minister to those who do live in fear of demons, assuring them that whether demons are real or only "imaginary" the mercy of God in Jesus Christ can and does put the demons or the images to rout, leaving no room on the battlefield for anything but sheer unyielding grace.

CHAPTER 4

The Miracle
of the
Resurrection

The resurrection of Jesus of Nazareth from the dead is the central miracle of the Christian faith. It plays a major role in each of the Gospels, and Paul, who pays no attention to the miracles which Jesus performed during his ministry, stresses the fundamental significance of the resurrection time and again. Indeed, apart from the faith in Jesus' resurrection it seems hard to imagine that there would be any Christian faith at all. Traditionally, at least, that miracle is at the very heart of Christian conviction.

Resurrection: Fact and Faith

Like belief in the other biblical miracles, belief in Jesus' resurrection from the dead involves both an assessment of the "facts" and an act of faith. Various Christians analyze the relationship between the events of Jesus' resurrection and the resurrection faith in various ways.

1. Some Christians think that the Christian faith is essentially the belief that certain historical events actually occurred. Foremost among these events is the event of Jesus' resurrection. Faith is faith in the *fact* that the tomb was empty and that Jesus appeared to various people. Faith is faith in the *fact* that he was dead and then was alive again.

2. Other Christians maintain that faith is faith in something larger than the historical facts. Faith is, perhaps, faith in the power of the living Lord. However, these Christians say, the historical facts *prove* the validity of that larger faith. Correctly understood, the evidence concerning the empty tomb and the appearances of Jesus demonstrates that Jesus has conquered death and is the living Lord of the world, the church, and the individual Christian. In technical language, the evidence is both necessary and sufficient to prove the validity of the faith.

3. Other Christians agree that the resurrection faith is faith in something larger than the historical facts. They may agree that faith is faith in the power of the living Lord. However, these Christians maintain that not even the evidence of the empty tomb and the appearances can *prove* that Jesus is the living Lord. These facts do provide clues which point in that direction. Furthermore these clues are an essential part of the resurrection faith, though they are not the heart of it. In technical language, these Christians maintain that the historical evidence is necessary but not sufficient for the faith to be valid.

4. Still other Christians agree that faith is faith in something larger than the historical facts and that the resurrection faith is faith in the power of the living Lord. However, for these Christians the question of what happened on the third day after the crucifixion is only incidental to the resurrection faith. Faith is a matter of our own personal direction toward Jesus the risen Lord or of the church's relationship to him, or faith is a matter of perceiving the risen Lord's activity in the world. Faith is therefore not dependent on the findings of historical research. The evidence in the New Testament cannot establish faith, and presumably new historical evidence could not harm faith, either.

5. Some Christians hold that the reliance on historical fact is an actual hindrance to real faith. Faith, to be faith, requires precisely the freedom from questions or proof, facticity, historicity. Faith which is dependent on this evidence is both too fragile and too timid to be faith. It is too fragile because it is threatened by the results of historical research. What seems safe and certain today could too easily be destroyed by what the historian or the archaeologist discovers tomorrow. Such faith is too timid because it demands evidence, like poor Thomas who insisted on seeing the wounds of the risen Lord with his own eyes. Real faith would take

the risk which is central to faith. It would not rely on facts or evidence. Even to raise the question of what "really happened" is a sign of unfaith.

Resurrection Stories and Other Miracle Stories

There are clearly various options for the Christian who tries to relate fact to faith in dealing with the resurrection. Our discussion of the relationship of fact and faith in other New Testament miracle stories may at least give us some clues to a more adequate view of the meaning of Jesus' resurrection than those we have discussed in the previous section. Let us look first at the similarities between the miracle stories and the resurrection stories.

Similarities

First, our discussion of miracles suggests the necessity and even the centrality of *events* as part of the way in which God deals with humankind. In the biblical faith God really acts in human history. We cannot reduce him to a deity who *might* behave with love or judgment, if he acts. Throughout the Bible, and especially in the incarnation, God *does* act. In the miracle stories, especially, events are attributed to the activity of God. Certainly the central miracle of resurrection implies that God really *did* something. The resurrection stories are not just illustrative of God's general qualities. They represent his specific, historical activity. Inescapably, the Christian faith is linked to history, for all its fragility. If, for instance, historians could provide evidence that Jesus of Nazareth had never existed or that someone else had been crucified in his place, Christianity would be exposed as a pious fraud. So, too, questions of historical evidence are not irrelevant to the faith in Jesus' resurrection.

However, just as the miracle stories are always more than stories of odd events, so, too, the resurrection faith is not just the belief in a number of facts. The faith in miracle is always a faith in God's activity. It requires going beyond the recital of what happened to the affirmation that what happened was the work of God, part of his saving activity. The faith in miracles requires interpretation. So, too, the resurrection faith is not just the belief that there was an empty tomb or that Jesus appeared to various people. The facts alone give us only a mysterious disappearance followed by mysterious appearances of a resuscitated corpse or an elusive ghost. The sermons in the book of Acts make clear that the early church moved beyond the facts to make a statement of faith: "This Jesus *God* raised up" (Acts 2:32). The claim that the resurrection is an act of God is the typical claim which the believer makes about a miracle. Such a claim is in part an interpretation. It is in part an act of faith.

Differences

Although we can interpret the resurrection in the light of other miracles, there are some differences between the resurrection stories and the other miracle stories which must inform our interpretation.

First, the resurrection event is such an extraordinary event that it sometimes seems to be *almost* outside history. As the creation, which brought forth being from nothingness, stands outside history, so resurrection, which brought forth life from death, seems almost to break out of the possibilities of historical existence. (Paul relates the two "events" in Romans 4:17.) Jesus' resurrection does not simply exceed expectation; it reverses expectation. It defies the fundamental reality of death and therefore stands in tension with everything we assume to be possible.

Second, we suggested in dealing with miracles that miracles are often events for which alternative explanations are possible. One kind of explanation we called "scientific" the other "personal." We suggested that each kind of explanation has its own kind of richness. Each is useful in its own way. However when it comes to the resurrection, the so-called "scientific" explanations do not explain; they explain away. As early as Matthew's Gospel, opponents of the Christians explained the empty tomb by saying that Jesus' disciples had stolen the body (Matthew 28:13). Explanations which claim that the resurrection faith was the result of hallucination or of a "Passover Plot"[1] do not really explain a resurrection. They explain an *apparent* resurrection. Resurrection, the radical reversal from death to life, *is* a radical reversal of everything which "scientific" explanations would lead us to expect. There are a variety of theological interpretations, a variety of ways of relating the evidence to the Christian faith. Non-theological explanations, however, do not explain the same event that theological explanations explain.

Third, and finally, the resurrection is central to the New

Testament witness in a way that none of the miracle stories is central. It is not so much a part of the Christian story as it is the fundamental presupposition of the Christian story. Therefore it is especially incumbent upon us to try to understand as fully as we can the variety and the unity of the New Testament understanding of resurrection.

Resurrection as a Clue to the Meaning of Miracle

The resurrection also enriches our understanding of other miracles by making clear that sometimes God works in ways which are unexpected and astonishing.

A central feature of the resurrection event in the New Testament is that it was utterly surprising. The disciples (though the Gospels suggest that they were forewarned) were astonished, and even when they saw the risen Lord, some did not believe (Matthew 28:17). Resurrection was astonishing because it stood against the clearest law by which we operate our lives: death is irreversible. In the resurrection the expectation that death had separated the believers from Jesus was reversed. The expectation that the hoped-for kingdom was doomed to defeat was reversed. The expectation that from now on life would have to continue without point or purpose was reversed.

Resurrection therefore stands over against law, over against the despairing certainty that there is nothing new. Richard R. Niebuhr rightly discerns that the belief in resurrection over against law is at the heart of the church's life:

> The conflict is between the interpretation of the community's history, and, ultimately, the history of Christendom, in terms of law or of resurrection. . . . The opposition between these two terms, law and resurrection, is complete, for even when it is used as an analogy or interpretative key, the resurrection cannot be converted into a generalization; it remains a single and arbitrary and wholly spontaneous event, just as every historical event does when it is taken by itself. It is the logical implicate of no principle; it can be inductively inferred from no grounds whatsoever.[2]

This understanding of resurrection reflects on our understanding of miracles. For Jesus' opponents the problem with Jesus' miracles was often precisely that they broke the laws, not scientific "laws" as we know them, but religious laws. Jesus (and God) was supposed to be bound by human expectations. God was not expected to do anything new. (See especially John 5:17-18; Mark 3:1-6.) For us, the problem with miracles is not so much that they violate some carefully rational scheme of "science" by which we live. It is that they evade our calculation, our prudent estimates of what is possible. They make life more difficult because they make life more astonishing. They surprise us when we prefer not to be surprised.

We suggested above that miracles may not be inexplicable events but may rather be events which are subject to alternative explanations. Sometimes the "personal" or theological explanation is richer than the "objective" explanation. One reason for this richness now becomes clear. The personal explanation leaves us open to the possibility that God who has acted will act again. This explanation has a predictive richness which the more objective accounts lack precisely because it predicts that human lives or human history may include what is genuinely astonishing and new.

Resurrection as the Basis for the Stress on Jesus' Miracles

Jesus was by no means the only miracle worker in the early centuries of our era. Both Judaism and Graeco-Roman culture provide us with examples of people who performed impressive miracles. Jesus' miracles are particularly important to the Christian because they are *his* miracles. Jesus is centrally important for the Christian because the Christian confesses him to be Lord, the revelation of God's activity in human life. For the early church, at least, it was the resurrection which validated Jesus' lordship.

Apart from his resurrection, Jesus presumably would have been remembered only as another wandering miracle worker, an impressive teacher who suffered an untimely death. Because of his resurrection, Jesus was (and is) honored and followed as the Son of God. Therefore his miracles take on special significance, given the resurrection. They are clearly acts which reveal the way in which God relates to history. In a particular way they are God's acts. Jesus' resurrection makes this clear. Therefore precisely because of the resurrection, we read the miracle stories with renewed and special interest.

Because the resurrection is the central miracle in the New Testament, we need to look with some care at the resurrection accounts to see what themes they stress. There are obviously differences and discrepancies among the accounts. We shall try to

face the difficulties which these pose for any historical reconstruc-
tion. At the same time we shall recognize that the variety of the
accounts is itself a testimony to the richness and variety of the New
Testament faith in resurrection.

CHAPTER **5**

Resurrection Traditions in the New Testament

The resurrection accounts in the New Testament are concerned both with the facts and with faith. In this chapter we shall try to discover what events the various New Testament writers recount and to see what significance they attached to those events. In the next chapter we shall try to deal more systematically with the significance of the resurrection in the New Testament's understanding of faith.

The Resurrection Account in 1 Corinthians 15:3-9

Paul's account of the resurrection is clearly the earliest account in the New Testament. Paul wrote First Corinthians before any of the Gospels had been written, and in this section of First Corinthians he is evidently quoting a tradition which precedes the epistle and precedes his own conversion to Christianity: "For I delivered to you . . . what I also received . . ." (15:3). The terms "deliver" and "receive" are terms which the rabbis use to refer to material which is carried in the oral tradition, and we therefore have a clear indication here that Paul is recalling traditional material to the Corinthians.

The traditional account which he quotes is this:

... that Christ died for our sins in accordance with the scriptures, that he was buried, that he was raised on the third day in accordance with the scriptures, and that he appeared to Cephas, then to the twelve. Then he appeared to more than five hundred brethren at one time, most of whom are still alive, though some have fallen asleep. Then he appeared to James, then to all the apostles (15:3-7).

Then Paul goes on to add: "Last of all, as to one untimely born, he appeared also to me" (15:8).

This passage and the argument of First Corinthians

Before looking at this resurrection tradition, we need to understand the reason why Paul feels called upon to quote the tradition at this point in First Corinthians.

It is clear that the belief in Jesus' resurrection is a belief which Paul and the Corinthians share. The Corinthians have received this tradition which Paul quotes and have believed it.

The problem is not that they deny the reality of Jesus' resurrection. The problem is that they deny the reality of their own future resurrection. They seem to think that all the promises of the gospel are already theirs in their present life: "Already you are filled! Already you have become rich!" (4:8). They seem to think that the Christian hope is limited to earthly life, and Paul holds that their faith is totally inadequate: "If for this life only we have hoped in Christ, we are of all men most to be pitied" (15:19).

Paul insists that Christ's resu   n indicates that there is a general resurrection. "Now if Chr.   ￿ preached as raised from the dead, how can some of you say that there is no resurrection of the dead?" (15:12). Christ's resurrection is not an isolated incident for Paul. It is the first instance of what will be a general resurrection. Paul believed that the age to come would include the resurrection of the dead. Christ's resurrection proves that the general resurrection has begun, and that the age to come is on its way.

Moreover, Paul sees Christ as a representative man. What Christ does, he does not just for himself but for all people. "For as in Adam all die, so also in Christ shall all be made alive" (15:22). Because the Corinthians see Jesus' resurrection as an isolated and unrepeatable event, they fail to understand the full significance of the resurrection faith

We can only stress ag   it what is at stake here is not Paul's (or the Corinthians'!) belief in Jesus' resurrection. That belief is the given to which Paul can appeal. What is at stake is the Corinthians' faith or lack of faith in the general resurrection of the dead, and Paul uses their belief in Jesus' resurrection as the grounds for his larger argument.

The tradition which Paul received

We have already pointed out that Paul's reference to Jesus' appearance to Paul himself was obviously added to the traditional material Paul was quoting (15:8). Further, it looks as though 15:6b, which says of the five hundred, "most . . . are still alive, though some have fallen asleep," is an addition by Paul, who is buttressing the tradition by referring to witnesses who are still alive and can presumably be questioned.[1] This means that the traditional formula originally read something like this:

> That Christ died for our sins in accordance with the scriptures,
> that he was buried, that he was raised on the third day in accordance with the scriptures,
> and that he appeared to Cephas, then to the twelve, and afterward to more than five hundred brethren at one time,
> then he appeared to James, then to all the apostles.

Several features of this tradition are essential to our understanding of this early statement about the resurrection.

1. The statement is already a theological statement and not simply an historical statement. It is a statement of faith, not just of facts. It is a statement of fact that Christ died. It is a statement of faith that "Christ died for our sins."

It is faith which interprets both Jesus' death and his resurrection as occurring "in accordance with the scriptures." The early church from the beginning was concerned to show that the Old Testament, perceived through faith, pointed to Jesus' crucifixion and resurrection. Furthermore the tradition uses the so-called "reverential passive," "He *was* raised on the third day, according to the scripture." Jews often used this passive form to refer to God's activity without using the name of God himself. Therefore what the formula implies is that "God raised him on the third day." (See Acts 2:24.) Therefore the tradition goes beyond the recitation of events, even of astonishing events like Jesus' rising, to attribute those events to the activity of God.

2. The formula seems to cite three central events: (a) "that Christ died for our sins according to the scriptures," (b) "that he was buried and that he was raised on the third day, according to the

scriptures," and (c) "that he appeared to Cephas" and so on.

A good deal of Protestant scholarship has maintained that the tradition of the appearances and the tradition of the empty tomb were originally passed on independently of one another.[2]

Scholars have maintained that the reference to Jesus' burial and resurrection in 1 Corinthians 15:4 does not indicate any knowledge of the tradition of the empty tomb.[3] However, the possibility that I Corinthians 15:4 may be a reference to the empty tomb tradition helps answer two difficult questions of interpretation. First, why the reference to burial at all? As Reginald Fuller says, it is hardly necessary to cite the burial as proof that Jesus was really dead. The previous verse, 15:3, makes clear that he was really dead, and there is no evidence that the earliest Christian apologetic had to prove that fact.[4] It is not at all clear why the burial tradition should have any particular place in a traditional confession of faith unless it had some sort of particular theological significance. Second, why the reference to resurrection on "the third day" in 15:4*b*? Fuller's complicated discussion of the possibilities proceeds on the assumption that there is no reference to the empty tomb tradition in 1 Corinthians 15.[5] However, other (later) writings indicate that references to "the third day" in the tradition sometimes were references to the story of the empty tomb. Matthew 27:64 and Luke 24:1-9 especially indicate that the reference to the third day was used as part of the empty tomb tradition.

Admittedly the evidence that 1 Corinthians 15:4 refers to the empty tomb tradition is by no means conclusive, and the phrase "in accordance with the scriptures" of 15:4 has still to be explained satisfactorily. However, the simplest explanation for the presence of 15:4 in the traditional affirmation seems to be that it alludes to the empty tomb tradition as 15:5 and following refer to the appearance tradition. Of course, the appearance tradition is far more important to Paul since it is an appearance of the risen Lord which validates his own apostleship.

3. The list of those to whom Christ appeared has some interesting features. First it seems to be an almost universal feature of the tradition that Peter (here listed with his Aramaic name, Cephas) was at least the first of the original disciples to witness the resurrection. In Mark 16:7 Peter is singled out from the other disciples for special mention. In Luke 24:34 the disciples report, "The Lord has risen indeed, and has appeared to Simon," before he

appears to the rest of them. In John 20:6-7, although the other disciple (presumably the author's favorite) outruns Peter and reaches the tomb first, it is Peter who first enters it and in that sense becomes the first witness to the fact of Jesus' resurrection. It seems quite likely that Peter's great authority in the early church derives from the fact that he was the first witness of the resurrection. (James's authority may derive in part from the fact that he is a resurrection witness and in part from the fact that he was Jesus' brother.)[6]

Second, against the assertion that the risen Lord appeared only to believers, this formula as Paul expands it makes clear that resurrection appearances were granted to at least one and probably two nonbelievers. Paul was obviously not a believer at the time that the risen Lord appeared to him. There is no evidence that James, Jesus' brother, was a believer either, and it is more likely that he was among those of Jesus' family who generally opposed Jesus' mission (see Mark 3:31). Therefore these two nonbelievers came both to faith and to status in the community through the resurrection appearances.

The appearance to Paul

Paul adds to the traditional quotation an assertion about himself: "Last of all, as to one untimely born, he appeared also to me" (1 Corinthians 15:8). The term for "he appeared" is exactly the same term which the tradition uses in referring to the appearances to Peter, the twelve, and the others. Therefore Paul does not wish to make any distinction between the resurrection appearances to other witnesses and the resurrection appearance to him. The only difference between his experience and theirs is that his came later.[7]

This leads to the question of whether the accounts of Paul's vision of the risen Lord give us any clues to the nature of Jesus' other resurrection appearances. Again we need to recall that First Corinthians was written before any of our Gospels were written.

Willi Marxsen claims that we can compare 1 Corinthians 15:8 to Galatians 1:15-16 to help us understand the nature of Paul's experience of the risen Lord.[8] The Galatians passage says:

> But when he who had set me apart before I was born, and had called me through his grace, was pleased to reveal his Son to [en] me, in order that I might preach him among the Gentiles, I did not confer with flesh and blood.

It might seem that this passage gives a clue to the nature of Paul's experience of the risen Lord. If so, we must admit that Paul does not refer to any visual experience in this passage, and one could perhaps argue that Paul's reference to "appearance" in 1 Corinthians 15:8 was dictated by the traditional material which Paul has just quoted, with its references to "appearances" to Peter and the rest. If that is the case, then Paul's experience may not have been an "appearance" of the risen Lord at all.

However, the passage in Galatians may not refer to the *content* of Paul's experience. The passage may rather refer to the status and the mission which that experience conferred upon him. It may be that the passage says that God has chosen to reveal his Son "by means of" Paul as Paul preaches to the Gentiles. This would certainly make sense in the context: "[God] was pleased to reveal his Son [by means of] me, in order that I might preach him among the Gentiles."[9]

More apposite therefore is the claim in 1 Corinthians 9:1a: "Am I not free? Am I not an apostle? Have I not seen Jesus our Lord?" Here Paul is not bound by any traditional context and yet speaks of his experience in terms which are unmistakably visual: he has *seen* the Lord.

The accounts of the Damascus Road experience in Acts may give *some* evidence of the nature of Paul's experience of the risen Lord, and therefore, by extension, some evidence of the nature of the other resurrection appearances. The tendency in recent scholarship is to regard the accounts of Paul in Acts as being more indicative of Luke's theology than of Paul's biography.[10] However, Reginald Fuller tries to discern in the three Damascus Road passages (Acts 9:1-22; 22:3-21; 26:1-23) evidences of a tradition which does not fit Luke's theological premises and which therefore has some claim to represent more accurate material about Paul's experience. Fuller concludes that:

> All three accounts, therefore, agree that in the Damascus road encounter there was a visionary element and an auditory element, and that the inner meaning of the encounter was apprehended by Paul alone. It would be safe to infer that these three common elements are pre-Lucan, not redactional.[11]

We can at least say this of Paul's experience of the resurrection. He did not distinguish it qualitatively from resurrection appearances to other witnesses like Peter. He describes it (and Acts describes it) at some points at least in terms which imply a visual experience. He nowhere indicates that he saw a Jesus who looked largely like the preresurrection Jesus, and the Acts accounts suggest that this is precisely what Paul did not see. However, what Paul saw and heard was identifiably Jesus. The accounts suggest that what happened was not just that Paul came to faith in Jesus but that Jesus came to Paul and that Paul knew who he was.

Jesus' resurrection body and our resurrection bodies

In 1 Corinthians 15 Paul goes to considerable trouble to describe the post-resurrection body of the believers:

> But some one will ask, "How are the dead raised? With what kind of body do they come?" You foolish man! What you sow does not come to life unless it dies. And what you sow is not the body which is to be, but a bare kernel, perhaps of wheat or of some other grain. But God gives it a body as he has chosen, and to each kind of seed its own body. . . . So is it with the resurrection of the dead. What is sown is perishable, what is raised is imperishable. It is sown in dishonor, it is raised in glory. It is sown in weakness, it is raised in power. It is sown a physical body, it is raised a spiritual body. If there is a physical body, there is also a spiritual body. Thus it is written, "The first man Adam became a living being"; the last Adam became a life-giving spirit. But it is not the spiritual which is first but the physical, and then the spiritual. The first man was from the earth, a man of dust; the second man is from heaven. As was the man of dust, so are those who are of dust; and as is the man of heaven, so are those who are of heaven. Just as we have borne the image of the man of dust, we shall also bear the image of the man of heaven (15:35-49).

The metaphysics is a little unclear, but the point is clear enough. After the resurrection the believers will still be identifiably themselves. They will be "bodies," recognizable and separate individuals. But they will not be the same old selves. They will be "spiritual bodies," participating in a new glory.

Does Paul therefore want to indicate that the case for Jesus is the same as it will be for the believer? Was Jesus resurrected as a spiritual body—identifiably himself but strikingly different from what he had been?

I think the evidence indicates that Paul would want to hold that Jesus, too, has been raised as a spiritual body.

First, the whole argument of 1 Corinthians 15 is that Jesus is *not* a unique case. He is the first fruit of the general resurrection, and what is true of him will be true of others. Presumably one can argue backwards that what is true of the general resurrection was also true of Jesus' resurrection. He was raised a "spiritual body."

Second, the passage we have just quoted again makes clear that Paul's reference to the resurrection bodies of believers as spiritual bodies is based precisely on an analogy with Jesus. "As was the man of dust, so are those who are of the dust; and as is the man of heaven, so are those who are of heaven. Just as we have borne the image of the man of dust, we shall also bear the image of the man of heaven" (1 Corinthians 15:48-49). The context makes clear that the image we shall bear is the image of the "spiritual body." Jesus therefore presumably arose as a spiritual body to whose image the believers will be conformed.

Further, as Fuller points out,[12] Philippians 3:20-21 supports the analogy between the resurrection body of Jesus and the resurrection body of the believer: "But our commonwealth is in heaven, and from it we await a Savior, the Lord Jesus Christ, who will change our lowly body to be like his glorious body, by the power which enables him even to subject all things to himself."

The evidence is therefore overwhelming that Paul believes that Jesus arose as a "spiritual body," as identifiably himself, but not as the same old self. The Jesus who rose was "glorified." His body could not simply be identified with that physical body which had died.

This insight fits well with our suggestion in the preceding paragraphs that in his own apprehension of the risen Lord, Paul did not claim to see Jesus in the physical body of his earthly ministry. Paul's experience involved *seeing* and what he saw was identifiably Jesus, but there is no indication that it looked like a resuscitated corpse or even a manlike ghost. He saw the glorified Jesus whose appearance presumably cannot be reduced to words, not even Paul's words, and certainly not ours.

In summation we can say that the earliest tradition about the resurrection, as we find it in 1 Corinthians 15, already includes both a recitation of events and a theological interpretation of those events. It probably contains a reference to the tradition of the empty tomb. It certainly contains references to Jesus' appearances to a number of believers and probably at least one unbeliever, James. It indicates that the first appearance, at least among church leaders, was to Peter.

Paul adds to this tradition the affirmation of his own authority as a resurrection witness. The New Testament accounts of Paul's Damascus Road experience suggest that while he had a real, visual experience of an identifiable Jesus, he did not see a resuscitated body or an identifiable ghost. Paul's own discussion of the resurrection bodies of believers confirms the belief that what he saw was Jesus glorified. Beyond that we cannot go safely.

Paul cites this material on resurrection, not to convince the Corinthians of the reality of Jesus' resurrection, but to argue from the belief in Jesus' resurrection, which they share, to the conclusion that there will also be a future general resurrection of the dead.

Preaching on the resurrection in 1 Corinthians 15

1. This passage is central to our understanding of the relationship of Christ's resurrection to our hopes for ourselves and for human history. It speaks particularly to those Christians who believe in Jesus' resurrection but believe that that was an absolutely unique event and holds no particular promise for others. Paul insists that Jesus' resurrection is the first fruit of a general resurrection and therefore a promise of hope for us all.

2. This passage makes particularly clear that Christ's resurrection was not simply an amazing event but a miracle. That is, it was an act of God, and it is a sign of God's final sovereignty over all the forces of evil.

3. For those who want to make Easter the celebration of natural renewal or God's general tendency to bring new life, First Corinthians is a reminder of the specificity of Jesus' resurrection. He was raised on the third day and appeared to identifiable, historical people.

4. Finally, the account of the appearance to Paul himself is a reminder that the risen Christ can call the most unlikely people and choose them to serve him.

The Resurrection Account in the Gospel of Mark

The earliest written account of the resurrection after Paul's account is found in Mark's Gospel. As Paul stresses the resurrection appearances, Mark's story stresses the finding of the empty tomb.

The odd ending of Mark's Gospel

In the earliest manuscripts, Mark's Gospel ends most abruptly: "And [the women] went out and fled from the tomb; for trembling and astonishment had come upon them; and they said nothing to any one, for they were afraid" (Mark 16:8).

To those familiar with the other Gospels, Mark's Gospel seems to leave out the accounts of the resurrection appearances and therefore to be strangely incomplete. Even in terms of Mark's Gospel this seems an odd place to end. If the women never told anyone, how did the resurrection faith arise and how did the writer of Mark know what had gone on?

Grammatically, too, the ending is odd. The word with which the last sentence ends (*gar*, "for") occurs much more frequently in the middle of a sentence than at the end. It is unusual to find the word at the end of a paragraph and exceedingly unusual to find it at the end of a book.

The longer endings of Mark, however, have small claim to validity. Mark 16:9-20 which the King James Version includes in the Gospel and the RSV gives in the notes is found only in later manuscripts of the Gospel. Its vocabulary is different from that of the rest of Mark's Gospel, and it seems to be a kind of pastiche made up of bits and pieces from the other Gospels. The so-called shorter ending cited in the notes of the RSV is found only in a few later manuscripts.

Furthermore, Matthew and Luke, who are presumably using Mark's version of the resurrection story, diverge from one another and go their separate ways after Mark 16:8. This suggests that their versions of Mark (or at least the version used by one of them) ended with 16:8. Therefore all the evidence indicates that, very early on, Mark 16:8 was the ending of the Gospel and that later Christian writers added the other endings.

Some scholars are still dissatisfied with the present ending of Mark's Gospel and think that the original ending must be missing. Perhaps Mark was interrupted in mid-sentence and never returned to his work, or he died before he could complete his work, or very early in its history the ending of the (only?) copy of the Gospel broke off the scroll and was forever lost.[13]

Other scholars like Lightfoot, Lohmeyer, and Marxsen maintain, for various reasons, that the present ending is an appropriate conclusion to Mark's Gospel and fits well with his theological concerns.[14] I am inclined to accept this latter view, though my understanding of the place of Mark 16:1-8 in Mark's Gospel is original, if not idiosyncratic.

Mark 16:1-8 and its place in Mark's theology

The following argument certainly does not represent a consensus of current scholarly opinion, but a new attempt to solve the problem. It is not clear that there *is* a consensus of scholarly opinion on the place of this passage in Mark's theology, but several scholars, at least, think that the injunction in 16:7, "But go, tell his disciples and Peter that he is going before you to Galilee; there you will see him, as he told you," is a reference to Jesus' Parousia and encouragement to the believers to keep an eye out for the Second Coming.[15]

It is generally agreed that Mark 16:7 refers to Mark 14:28 and that both of these verses have been added by Mark to the traditional material of Mark 14:26-31 and Mark 16:1-8, which he uses.[16]

> "But after I am raised up, I will go before you to Galilee" (Mark 14:28).
> "But go, tell his disciples and Peter that he is going before you to Galilee; there you will see him, as he told you" (Mark 16:7).

Granted that Mark added these references to Jesus' "going before" the disciples to Galilee, what does he mean by these references?

From Lohmeyer on there has been general agreement that Galilee and Jerusalem serve not just geographical but theological functions in Mark's Gospel.[17] The first section of the Gospel, through about 10:31, is set in Galilee. The last section of the Gospel is set in Jerusalem. Jerusalem is important because it is the location for Jesus' suffering and death. The theological importance of Galilee has not seemed so clear.

The beginning of the "Jerusalem" section of Mark's Gospel has a striking similarity to the passage in 16:7 (or 14:28). Only here and in 14:28 and 16:7 Mark uses the verb *proago* (I go before).

> And they were on the road, going up to Jerusalem, and Jesus was walking ahead [*proago*] of them; and they were amazed, and those who followed were afraid. And taking the twelve again, he began to tell them what was to happen to him, saying, "Behold, we are going up to Jerusalem; and the Son of man will be delivered to the chief priests and the scribes, and they will condemn him to death, and deliver him to the Gentiles; and they will mock him, and spit upon him, and scourge him, and kill him; and after three days he will rise" (Mark 10:32-34).

This seems clearly to be a Markan construction with a particular theological intent. It is not just that Jesus is preceding the disciples to the geographical Jerusalem. Jesus is preceding them (and the readers) into the Jerusalem section of the Gospel, and as he goes he is explaining to the disciples (and to the readers) the significance of the Jerusalem section of the Gospel. It is the place where Jesus' betrayal, conviction, death (and resurrection) will take place. The disciples are filled with fear.

Both 14:28 and 16:7 are similar theological constructions. In the one place Jesus, in the other the young man, explain that Jesus precedes the disciples—not just into the geographical Galilee, but into the "Galilee" section of the Gospel (chapters 1-10). They explain to the followers that *there,* in the Galilee section of the Gospel, they will "see" the risen Lord. Just as 10:32-34 explains the function of the Jerusalem section of Mark's Gospel—that it is the locus for the passion, death, and empty tomb—so 16:7 (and 14:28) explains the function of the Galilee section of Mark's Gospel. It is the locus for the appearances of the risen and living Lord. Again the hearers are afraid! (16:8).

Mark's readers are therefore directed to look for the risen Lord, not in some further "appearance" stories to be added at the end of the Gospel, but in the stories which Mark has already told. They are directed back to the beginning of the Gospel. (We have already argued that Mark's Gospel is deliberately a book of secrets, filled with mysteries revealed only to the believing and alert reader. The meaning of the book itself becomes one of those mysteries, and the reminder of 16:7, "There you will see him," is in part a reminder to the reader to read the first ten chapters of the Gospel to understand the significance of the risen Lord and his relationship to the church.)

When the readers turn back to the beginning of the Galilee section of the Gospel (after the prologue at the Jordan), they find this story:

> And passing along by the Sea of Galilee, he saw Simon and Andrew the brother of Simon casting a net in the sea; for they were fishermen. And Jesus said to them, "Follow me, and I will make you become fishers of men." And immediately they left their nets and followed him (Mark 1:16-18).

Then the story goes on to relate the call of the sons of Zebedee. There are two other versions of this story in the Gospels. One version is found in John 21. There the risen Lord appears to Peter, the sons of Zebedee, and others by the Sea of Tiberias (or Galilee).

After the miraculous haul of fish and the reminder to Peter to feed Jesus' lambs, Jesus says to Peter: "Follow me!"

This story, which in John is clearly the story of a post-resurrection appearance, in Luke has been "historicized" as part of Jesus' ministry, but it still bears the clear marks of its original place as a post-resurrection story.[18] Luke 5:1-11 is again set at the sea (or lake). Again Simon and the sons of Zebedee are fishing. Again there is the miraculous haul of fish. Peter's reaction to Jesus is so awestruck that it suggests that originally this was the reaction to an epiphany of the risen Lord: "But when Simon Peter saw [the catch], he fell down at Jesus' knees, saying, 'Depart from me, for I am a sinful man, O Lord'" (Luke 5:8). The story in Luke includes a slightly different version of the call to Peter, which still clearly recalls Mark 1:17. "Do not be afraid; henceforth you will be catching men" (Luke 5:10). The story ends with another reference to "following." "And when they had brought their boats to land, they left everything and followed him" (Luke 5:11).

It seems quite possible that Mark 1:16-20 represents another deliberate placement of a traditional resurrection story in the "historical" ministry of Jesus. Mark's purpose, however, was not to historicize the stories of the risen Lord, but to enrich the stories of the historical Jesus by using them as the means by which he talked about the relationship of the risen Lord to the church. The Galilee section of the Gospel begins with a story in which the risen Lord called Peter, Andrew, and the sons of Zebedee. It goes on to show how the risen Lord continues to relate to the church which he has called.

There is some further confirmation that the call by the sea was originally a clear resurrection story in the fragment which follows the account of the empty tomb in the Gospel of Peter. "But I, Simon Peter, and my brother, took our nets and went to the sea. And there was with us Levi, the son of Alphaeus, whom the Lord. . . ." Unfortunately the Gospel breaks off here, but there is the implication that in the fuller Gospel the Lord then appeared to Simon and his brother by the sea. (Interestingly, for no apparent reason, in Mark 2:13-14 Jesus returns to the sea to teach and to call Levi, who in the Gospel of Peter was one of the disciples whom the risen Lord presumably met at the sea.)

We have already argued that Mark uses the miracle stories in the Galilee section of his Gospel to describe the relationship of the living Lord to the community of faith. We are now suggesting that the ending to Mark's Gospel is the place where Mark tells the reader that this is what he is going to do. The reader is directed to the Galilee section of Mark's Gospel to see the risen Jesus, to see what he continues to mean in the ongoing life of the church. When the reader turns to the Galilee section, the first story he finds is the story of the call of the disciples by the sea—a story which was originally the story of a post-resurrection epiphany. Far from ignoring the appearances of the living Lord, Mark's Gospel is full of them. They are found, however, not at the end of his Gospel but in its first section. Mark reworks the traditional sources about Jesus' ministry to make them reminders to the church of the way in which the risen Lord continues to be active and present in its life. (For a discussion of the way in which Mark reworks the miracle stories in terms of the resurrection, see pp. 39-42.)

"Historical" evidence on resurrection in Mark's Gospel

There are a few clues in Mark 16:1-8 to the question of "what happened" in the resurrection.

1. The tradition in this chapter is clearly pre-Markan. (We can see the way in which he revises it to fit his own theological concerns.) This means that at least very early in the church's tradition, the story of the empty tomb was told.

2. Women are here cited as the witnesses to the empty tomb. In those early and paternalistic days, women were not generally considered to have very high reliability as witnesses. If the early church had wanted to work up the best possible case for the accuracy of the empty tomb account, they would not have invented women as the witnesses. Therefore the fact that women are still cited as witnesses can only be because women were the earliest witnesses. (How sweet are the uses of scholarship: to return by so circuitous a route to so simple a conclusion.)

3. Both 14:28 and 16:7 would indicate that at least in our earliest Gospel it was understood that the resurrection appearances occurred in Galilee. Verse 14:27 indicates that the disciples had probably scattered from Jerusalem at the time of the arrest and crucifixion, leaving the women behind to witness the empty tomb. It was therefore to the disciples, scattered to Galilee, that the risen Lord first appeared.

Preaching on the resurrection in Mark

1. According to our interpretation, Mark 16:6-7 ("He has risen, he is not here. . . . But go, tell his disciples and Peter that he is going before you to Galilee; there you will see him.") is a reminder to the reader to reread the first part of Mark's Gospel. There he will find Mark's suggestions of the ways in which the living Lord continues to relate to the church.

With any interpretation, the verse is useful homiletically. It reminds us that we are not to stand around empty tombs, whether they be institutional, scholarly, or dogmatic, expecting to find Christ there. He goes before us into the future. More than that, he goes before us to Galilee, which for the disciples was the place they lived their everyday lives among the people they knew. So the passage suggests that in the Galilees of our everyday lives we shall see and recognize the risen Lord.

2. Further, if our interpretation of Mark's Gospel is correct, then the entire first section of the Gospel, chapters 1-10, provides material for understanding the way in which the risen Christ relates to the community. This is not to say that we cannot derive valid historical information from Mark's Gospel. Nor is it to say that the first ten chapters of the Gospel are a series of post-resurrection appearances reshaped as part of Jesus' ministry. Rather, Mark has reshaped the tradition about Jesus' ministry. His purpose is not just to show what Jesus used to do, but what he is now doing. We can therefore try to understand what Mark was saying about the risen Lord's relationship to Mark's community. With some imagination we can try to translate Mark's understanding in order to understand the ways in which the risen Christ relates to our community.

The Resurrection Account in the Gospel of Matthew

Matthew uses Mark for his source up to the point where Mark ends at 16:8. Therefore we can get some idea of Matthew's special concerns by seeing the way in which he revises the material he takes from Mark.

Matthew's changes in the Markan material: Matthew 28:1-10

First, Matthew embellishes the miraculous features of the story. Matthew adds an earthquake to his description of the scene, and while Mark has a young man sitting at the tomb, Matthew has an angel descend from heaven to roll away the stone. (Matthew's tendency to augment the marvelous features of a scene is also evident when he tells of an earthquake and a resurrection of the saints at the time of the crucifixion 27:51-53.)

Second, we remember that in Mark 14:28 Jesus prophesies that his disciples will scatter but that he will go before them to Galilee. Then in Mark 16:7 the young man refers to that prophecy. Matthew keeps the prophecy of Mark 14:28 (Matthew 26:32), but in 28:7 he does not have the angel refer to it. Rather, the angel makes the announcement on his own authority: "Then go quickly and tell his disciples that he has risen from the dead, and behold, he is going before you to Galilee; there you will see him. Lo, I have told you." The reference to Jesus' preceding prediction may be unnecessary for Matthew, since Jesus appears to the women in 28:10 and again announces that he will appear in Galilee. Matthew likes angelic announcements anyway (see 1:20; 2:19-20), and it may be that he uses this device to underline the importance and authority of Jesus' own pronouncement in Matthew 28:10.

Third, Matthew omits the special reference to Peter in Mark 16:7 and simply has the angel instruct the women to tell all the disciples that Jesus is going to Galilee. This is certainly not because Matthew wishes to downgrade Peter's special status (see Matthew 16:18-19). More likely it is because Matthew wishes to end his Gospel with the appearance to all the disciples (28:16-20) and either does not know or does not need to recount any special appearance to Peter.

Finally, Matthew omits Mark's report that the women said nothing to anyone (Mark 16:8). We have already noted (see p. 102) that this claim of Mark causes some historical and theological difficulties. In order to smooth out these difficulties, Matthew says that though the women were filled with fear, they were also filled with "great joy, and ran to tell his disciples" (Matthew 28:8).

The appearance to the women: Matthew 28:9-10

Mark's account breaks off with the parallel to Matthew 28:8. Matthew goes on to add an account of the appearance to the women. This seems to represent a tendency to bring together two originally distinct traditions—the tradition of an empty tomb in Jerusalem, which the women witnessed, and the tradition of appearances in Galilee, which the disciples witnessed.

Furthermore, in this passage Jesus gives explicit instructions for the disciples' trip to Galilee. Mark 16:7 in conjunction with Mark

14:27-28 gives the distinct (and probably accurate) impression that at the time of the crucifixion the disciples scattered to Galilee out of fear. Matthew is frequently concerned with elevating Mark's rather low view of the disciples' faithfulness, so he insists that the disciples did not go to Galilee out of fear, but in response to a direct command from the risen Lord.

The apologetic concern with the empty tomb: Matthew 27:62-66; 28:11-15

These stories appear only in Matthew and indicate that the debate over what had happened to Jesus' body was still a lively debate in Matthew's community. Probably Matthew was written in a community where the church and the synagogue lived in continuing and bitter dialogue, and Matthew is defending the resurrection faith against the repeated claim that Jesus' body had been stolen from the tomb.

The story of the setting of the guard in Matthew 27:62-66 is told to show that it would have been impossible for the disciples to steal Jesus' body. The story of the bribing of the soldiers in Matthew 28:11-15 is told to show why the report that Jesus' body was stolen has arisen all the same.

The appearance in Galilee: Matthew 28:16-20

While it seems altogether likely that the earliest traditions maintain that the risen Jesus appeared to the disciples in Galilee, it is equally likely that this particular scene is a Matthean construction.

Both the setting of the scene and its content show specifically Matthean concerns.

For Matthew, the mountain where the appearance occurs is the place where Jesus as the new Moses provides the right interpretation of the new Torah (Matthew 5:1; also see Matthew 17:1; 24:3). Here Jesus appears on the mountain to sum up that new Torah.

The themes in this scene are also typically Matthean. The theme of faith and unfaith, so important throughout Matthew's Gospel, is still evident at its close. Despite the appearance of the risen Lord, some of the disciples still doubt (28:17). The contrast between faith and unfaith is clear.

Still other Matthean themes are evident in Jesus' last charge to the disciples (Matthew 28:18-20). Jesus' stress on his own authority

(28:18) recalls Matthew 5-9 where Matthew demonstrates to the reader Jesus' authority both as teacher and as healer. The call to make disciples recalls Jesus' authorizing of his disciples and his instructions on the meaning of discipleship in Matthew 10. The reference to "teaching" and "commanding" in Matthew 28:19 recalls the five great discourses of Matthew where Jesus presents the new Torah for Christians. The concluding reference to the "close of the age" (Matthew 28:20) recalls the Matthean emphasis on a final day of judgment when Jesus will return to judge all people on the basis of their obedience to the new Torah which he brings. (See especially Matthew 24-25.)

The content of Jesus' instructions to his disciples is therefore as important as the fact of the appearance itself. The point of this passage is not to prove the resurrection of Jesus. The point is to proclaim his authority, to announce his orders to the church, and to affirm the promise of his continuing presence. In remarkably short space, this passage makes clear what Matthew sees to be the *meaning* of Jesus' resurrection. Jesus' resurrection validates the great themes of Jesus' ministry and commissions the church to continue that ministry.

Excursus: the historicity of the empty tomb

Arguments against the historicity of the story of the empty tomb are generally based first on the assumption that the traditions concerning the empty tomb are comparatively late and second on the inherent improbability of the claim that Jesus' tomb was found empty.

Our study certainly raises some questions about the first assumption. It is at least possible that the earliest tradition we have concerning Jesus' resurrection (1 Corinthians 15:3-7) includes an implicit reference to the empty tomb (1 Corinthians 15:4). It is clear that the empty tomb story in Mark's Gospel (Mark 16:1-8) contained traditional material which Mark altered to reflect his own theological concern. The tradition of the empty tomb is therefore at least early enough to precede the writing of our earliest Gospel.

Moreover, the apologetic motif we have noted in Matthew's Gospel indicates that in the debate between Christians and Jews, at least in Matthew's community, the question was not *whether* the tomb was empty but *why* the tomb was empty. Had the tomb not been empty, it is hard to see why the whole debate about the stolen body should have arisen. The problem of improbability must therefore be restated. What strikes us as improbable is not that the tomb should have been empty, but that the tomb should have been empty for the reason the early Christians said it was empty: because Christ was risen.

We are stuck or blessed therefore with a clear paradigm of the problem of alternative explanations for the resurrection. In the case of the empty tomb, one explanation is that the disciples stole the body. If that explanation is correct, then the whole resurrection faith is at the very least suspect, since it is based in part on a fraud, however pious. The other traditional explanation is that God raised Jesus from the dead.

Of course the empty tomb is not sufficient to prove that God raised Jesus from the dead. The empty tomb is probably not even necessary for the belief in the resurrection. (Paul's belief, at least, was not based primarily on the empty tomb. It is conceivable that there might have been no empty tomb and still have been a resurrection faith.)

However, given the empty tomb (and historically it seems to be a given) it may be necessary for the Christian to explain the empty tomb as part of God's great act in raising Jesus Christ. It is hard to see how any other explanation is congruent with the fullness of the Christian faith. If some other explanation should prove accurate, then the faith would require some rethinking.

We are faced again with the fragile relationship between historical events and the affirmations of our faith.

Preaching on the resurrection in Matthew

1. Matthew's particular theological concerns appear especially in the story of the Great Commission (28:16-20). This story indicates the way in which the risen Lord gives both authority and responsibility to the church. The church is here authorized to carry on Jesus' own mission.

Moreover, the passage makes clear that the church does not carry on that mission apart from the promise of Christ's presence: "And lo, I am with you always, to the close of the age" (Matthew 28:20).

The content of the commission is evangelical, but it is evangelical in terms suitable to Matthew's concerns. The church is not just to make church members of all nations, it is to make *disciples* of all nations and to teach them to observe Jesus' commandments. That is, they are to be taught the new Torah and enlisted in the cause of the higher righteousness which Jesus proclaims.

The recollection in 28:17 that even when they saw the risen Lord "some doubted" is a healthy reminder that even when we have said all we can about the empty tomb and even when we are confronted by the risen Lord, it takes faith to know him for who he is.

2. Matthew's Gospel is the place where the argument about the empty tomb is carried on most explicitly and extensively. This material, however, seems to provide more grist for Bible study and discussion than for preaching, which is not really a matter of proving historical facts.

3. The reminder in Matthew 28:20 of the "close of the age" recalls the parables of Matthew 25 and reminds us that in Matthew, especially, the risen Christ will serve as judge of people and nations.

The Resurrection Account in Luke–Acts

Like Matthew, Luke used Mark as a source up to the point where Mark ends at 16:8.[19] He then makes several changes in the material.

Luke's changes in the Markan material: Luke 24:1-11

First, there are two men in dazzling apparel as opposed to the one man at the tomb in Mark (Luke 24:4; Mark 16:5). The reason for the pair of messengers is unclear, but probably they appear again to explain the ascension in Acts 1:10.[20]

Second, the two men begin with the question which contains at least an implicit pronouncement of the resurrection: "Why do you seek the living among the dead?" (Luke 24:5). This pronouncement may also be a reminder to Luke's church of the proper place to serve the living Lord, not by looking to the past, but by engaging in the present ministry of proclamation and service.

Third, for Luke the resurrection appearances occur in Jerusalem, and it is from Jerusalem that the church begins its mission. Therefore the prediction of resurrection appearances in Galilee (Mark 16:7) is drastically changed in Luke 24:6, where the young men say: "Remember how he told you while he was still in

Galilee. . . ." They then go on to remind the women of Jesus' passion and resurrection predictions.

Fourth, Luke omits Mark's reference to the women's fearful silence and has them go tell the eleven what has happened (24:9). This again gets around some of the difficulties in Mark's odd ending.

Finally, Luke gives an actual account of the women's report to the apostles. Again the problem of faith and doubt is evident even in the earliest church. Despite the women's report, the apostles did not believe.

Emmaus: Luke 24:13-35

This story occurs in Luke's Gospel only. It contains a number of theological motifs.

First, the theme of doubt is continued from 24:11. According to 24:24 some of the apostles went and found the empty tomb, as the women had reported. However, since the apostles did not see Jesus, the men on the road to Emmaus still did not believe. Luke indicates therefore that the empty tomb is not sufficient evidence for the resurrection faith. It takes (or at least took) the experience of the living Lord to bring forth that faith.

Second, the risen Christ serves as the first "Christian" interpreter of the Old Testament. It is only after the resurrection that the early Christians were able to understand that the Old Testament points toward Jesus' suffering and resurrection and indicates how all this "was necessary." This seems an accurate reflection of the way in which the church was first able to interpret the Old Testament in the light of Jesus' passion and resurrection only *after* the resurrection. It was the church's belief that the living Lord or the Holy Spirit guided the church in that new kind of interpretation of Scripture.

Third, this story again suggests the problem of recognition of the living Lord. The one who appeared to the men on the road was Jesus, but he was not just the same old Jesus, since "their eyes were kept from recognizing him" (24:16). Apparently it took a special gift of self-disclosure by Jesus before people were able to recognize him. (His sudden vanishing also indicates that this was not a resuscitated corpse, but something else—24:31.)

Fourth, the gift of self-disclosure comes in the breaking of the bread (Luke 24:30). As the language of that verse makes clear, this is a reference to the church's celebration of communion. It is still in the breaking of the bread that the risen Lord is revealed.

Finally, verse 34 preserves the tradition of the first appearance to Peter. When the men returned to the eleven, they were greeted with the announcement: "The Lord has risen indeed, and has appeared to Simon!" Note again that for Luke the *appearance* confirmed what the empty tomb alone could not. Christ is risen.

The appearance in Jerusalem: Luke 24:36-49

This material is found only in Luke and has several noteworthy features.

First, in verses 36-39 the physicality of the resurrection body is stressed as it is not in Mark or Paul (or in the Emmaus story, either). Jesus invites the eleven to handle him, declares that he has flesh and bones, and eats a piece of broiled fish as a clear demonstration of his physicality.

Second, as in the Emmaus story, the risen Lord is the interpreter of Old Testament Scripture to the church. Again Jesus stresses the *necessity (dei)* of what has happened to him (24:44). He makes clear that the purpose of his passion and resurrection is revealed in the Old Testament.

Third, this is a story of the founding of the church by Jesus himself. Jesus' speech picks up several Lukan themes: the fact that the church begins at Jerusalem and spreads from there; the role of the apostles as witnesses; the promise of power from on high. The scene is a prologue to Pentecost. Luke, of course, is the most concerned of the Gospel writers with the history of the church, and he sees that history beginning with the appearance of the risen Lord.

The geography and chronology of resurrection: Luke 24:50-53; Acts 1:1-11

There are a number of textual and critical problems with these passages.[21] Nevertheless we can perceive some dominant motifs. Assuming that the phrase, "and was carried up into heaven" (RSV footnote) in Luke 24:51 is original,[22] we apparently have two accounts of Jesus' "ascension."

The first account, in Luke 24:51, may well derive from the primitive Christian view that upon his resurrection Jesus was immediately assumed into heaven (see Acts 3:21) and that the resurrection appearances were appearances from heaven. (First Corinthians 15, especially Paul's reference to the appearance to him, would be consonant with such a view.) The second account, in Acts 1:9, reflects the later (Lukan?) view that the risen Lord continued his earthly epiphany for a period of forty days and was then raised into heaven to await the Second Coming.[23]

Whatever the origins of the two ascension accounts and the notion of forty days of appearances, Luke has objectified considerably the resurrection both chronologically and geographically.

For Mark and Paul the resurrection is an eschatological event, the first fruit of a new age. From that moment forward, the living Lord is active in the church, working toward the fullness of the kingdom. For Matthew, the risen Lord gives teaching authority to the church and remains with it until the end of the age. For Luke the resurrection is a transition between two ages, the age of Jesus' self-revelation and the age of the church. Jesus spends forty days preparing the disciples for Pentecost; then he returns to heaven to wait indefinitely for the Parousia. The new era begins with the coming of the Holy Spirit. More than any other New Testament writer, Luke makes the resurrection an event in history rather than an event which transcends and transforms history.

Luke objectifies his story geographically because he has objectified the resurrection appearances more than the other Gospel writers. Jesus is now flesh and bones and eats fish. That kind of physical body must be removed physically to a physical heaven on an actual cloud.

Jesus' farewell speech in Acts 1:7 and following reiterates Luke's concerns with the founding of the church. The apostles are to await the gift of the Holy Spirit, and they are to be Jesus' witnesses (again beginning in Jerusalem).

Finally, the passage in Acts reiterates Luke's stress on the delay of the Parousia. Jesus reminds the disciples: "It is not for you to know times or seasons which the Father has fixed by his own authority" (Acts 1:7). And the two men remind the gaping apostles that they had better get on with the business of establishing the church and not stand around waiting for Jesus: "Men of Galilee, why do you stand looking into heaven?" (Acts 1:11).

For Luke, therefore, the risen Lord instructs the church in the meaning of the Old Testament. He shows that the Old Testament points toward the necessity of his own passion and resurrection. He has a physical body and a temporal history as risen Lord. He plays a role in one more of God's acts within history. He then prepares the church for the gift and power of the Holy Spirit and for the beginning of its mission. Then he returns to heaven to await the Parousia and leaves the business of the church to the Holy Spirit.

Preaching on the resurrection in Luke–Acts

1. The question to the women at the empty tomb, "Why do you seek the living among the dead?" (Luke 24:5), and the question to the apostles at the ascension, "Men of Galilee, why do you stand looking into heaven?" (Acts 1:11), can both serve as healthy homiletic reminders that the church's business is primarily with this world and this time. Undue concern with the historical past or the heavenly hope could too easily distract us from serving Christ in our own time and place. Certainly Luke is especially concerned that the church be about its business, leaving the past and the future to the mercy of God.

2. The Emmaus story (Luke 24:13-35) in many ways provides a paradigm of the relationship of the believer to the risen Lord. It is especially helpful as a text for the Lord's Supper, reminding the congregation that we celebrate not just a memory but a presence. His presence informs our reflection on the past ("Did not our hearts burn within us?") and inspires us to action (as the Emmaus disciples rose immediately and returned to Jerusalem).

3. There is perhaps a sad reminder of the role women have played in Luke's church and ours. God in his free mercy has his messengers first proclaim to women the good news of Christ's resurrection (24:4ff.). All too typically the male apostles refuse to heed them: "But these words seemed to them an idle tale, and they did not believe them" (24:11).

4. For Luke, too, the risen Christ authorizes the mission of the church. The church is to carry out his ministry, under the guidance of the Holy Spirit, until his (long delayed) return (see especially Luke 24:48-49; Acts 1:7-8).

The Resurrection Account in John

Almost certainly John 21 was added to the Fourth Gospel after that Gospel was essentially complete. (Of course the tradition behind John 21 could still be as early or earlier than the Gospel itself.) John 20:30-31 brings the original book to a fitting close:

> Now Jesus did many other signs in the presence of the disciples, which are not written in this book; but these are written that you may believe that Jesus is the Christ, the Son of God, and that believing you may have life in his name.

Therefore we shall consider John 20 and John 21 separately.

The place of resurrection in John's theology

In John's Gospel the crucifixion more than the resurrection is the mark of Jesus' final triumph. The goal of his ministry is to return to the Father (see 14:28). The beginning of this return is the crucifixion, when Jesus is literally exalted, lifted up toward heaven:

> No one has ascended into heaven but he who descended from heaven, the Son of man. And as Moses lifted up the serpent in the wilderness, so must the Son of man be lifted up, that whoever believes in him may have eternal life (3:13-15).

Jesus accepts the cross because he recognizes the cross as the goal of his mission: "And what shall I say, 'Father, save me from this hour'? No, for this purpose I have come to this hour. Father, glorify thy name" (12:27-28; see also 10:18). In John's Gospel alone Jesus carries the cross to Golgotha without any help, and his final cry is not a cry of desolation but a cry of triumph: "It is finished" (19:30).

Furthermore, Jesus does not really require the resurrection in order to manifest his glory. His glory is complete only in his return to the Father, nevertheless that glory has been manifest throughout his mission, and the believers are those who can recognize and acknowledge that glory (1:14).

Therefore, for John the resurrection is neither Jesus' final triumph nor the manifestation of his glory. It serves rather a guaranteeing and a didactic function. It sets God's seal on the fact that Jesus is the Word made flesh, that he has manifested his glory among people. And it provides Jesus with the opportunity to make clear to his disciples and to John's readers the importance of the entire Gospel. Jesus stops en route to the Father in order to confirm his followers in their faith, to remind them of what they are called to believe, and to inspire them to be about the business of founding the church.

The accounts in John 20

John 20:1-18

We note, first, that the empty tomb and the appearance traditions are again conflated here. One of the women, Mary Magdalene, is still the first witness to the empty tomb; but two of the disciples also see the empty tomb, and at least one of them believes in the resurrection on the basis of the empty tomb (20:8). Then, as in Matthew (but unlike Mark and Luke), Jesus appears to a woman before appearing to the disciples.

Second, as Marxsen suggests, John 20:3-10 has probably been interpolated in the story of Mary Magdalene by the evangelist himself. The story preserves the priority of Simon Peter in a way congenial to the tradition, but at the same time gives special status to the beloved disciple, who is John's favorite witness.[24] The balance among the claims of Mary, Peter, and the beloved disciple is carefully weighed. Mary is the first to see that the stone has been taken away. The beloved disciple (outrunning Peter in his zeal) reaches the tomb first and looks in, but does not enter. Peter is the first to enter the tomb, so he has a modest priority. But the beloved disciple is still the first to believe (v. 8). John nods to the tradition while maintaining the special importance of the beloved disciple.

Third, we note again that the Jesus who appears to Mary Magdalene is not immediately recognizable as the Jesus she had known: "Saying this, she turned round and saw Jesus standing, but she did not know that it was Jesus" (John 20:14). Again the tradition suggests that while it was Jesus who was risen, it was not simply the same old Jesus the disciples had known. Mary finally recognizes him only by his word to her.

Finally, the passage indicates the guaranteeing and didactic function which the resurrection stories serve in John's Gospel. Jesus gives Mary the interpretation of what is happening: "Go to my brethren and say to them, I am ascending to my Father and your Father, to my God and your God." The puzzling command, "Do not hold me," can best be interpreted in the light of Jesus' didactic purpose. He has insisted elsewhere in the Gospel that it is good for the disciples that he should return to the Father. They should not mourn his departure, but should rejoice because his mission will then be complete, and because the Father will send the Holy Spirit (see 14:25-29). The command to Mary can best be translated: "Don't try to hold me." The point is that she (and other believers) are not to try to cling to the earthly Jesus or to mourn the end of his ministry. They are to rejoice in his return to the Father and to live under the ongoing guidance of the Paraclete.

John 20:19-23

The spectacular nature of the resurrection is here emphasized when the risen Lord appears despite the closed door (20:19).

When Jesus shows the disciples his hands and side, he confirms that it is really he, the crucified one, who is risen. More than that, his resurrection serves as a guarantee of the importance of his crucifixion. The risen one again makes manifest the marks of his final triumph.

As in John 14:27, Jesus bestows on the disciples the gift of peace. This is closely related to the gift of the Holy Spirit (20:19, 21-22). Again, the risen Lord indicates that his departure can be for the disciples' good, since he leaves with them the invaluable gift.

Finally, as in Matthew 28:16-20, the risen Christ here implicitly founds the church by giving the disciples the gift of the Holy Spirit and by bestowing upon them the authority to forgive sins (20:23).

John 20:24-29

The passage again stresses the identity of the risen Lord with the crucified Jesus. The insistence that Jesus is risen precisely as the crucified one underlines the centrality of the crucifixion as the central mark of Jesus' triumph in John's Gospel.

Thomas' demand to touch the risen Lord is like the recurring demand in the earlier part of the Gospel for signs. (See above, p. 60.) Here the request for a sign is granted. Jesus provides Thomas with "proof" of his resurrection. However, it is clear that it is better to believe without signs: "Have you believed because you have seen me? Blessed are those who have not seen and yet believe" (20:29). This word is a blessing on all those later Christians who must believe on the testimony of the disciples; and it is a blessing on the readers of John's Gospel, who must also believe without seeing.

Thomas, the doubter, makes the fullest Christological confession of the Gospel of John. The resurrection confirms for him the meaning of Jesus' entire ministry: "My Lord and my God!" (20:28).

The closing verses of the original book (20:30-31) reaffirm the evangelist's concern with the importance of signs. They call the reader to belief, and they promise eternal life to the believer.

The account in John 21

Although this chapter represents a later addition to the Gospel of John, the story it contains may be early.

We have already suggested that this is basically another version of the same story we find in Luke 5:1-11 and Mark 1:16-20. It represents a resurrection appearance in Galilee and may therefore precede the time when appearance stories were conflated with empty tomb stories and appearances which were located in Jerusalem.

The story has certainly been shaped by John's community. It includes yet another description of the relationship between Peter and the beloved disciple, and it includes the claim that that disciple is the witness whose testimony lies behind the chapter and perhaps behind the entire Gospel of John (21:24). Several themes emerge from the story.

First we note again that Jesus is not immediately recognizable to the disciples (21:4). Here it is not his word but the miracle he performs which confirms that he is the Lord (21:7). Again the story maintains a tenuous balance between the priority of Peter and the priority of the beloved disciple. It is the beloved disciple who first recognizes Jesus, but it is Peter who rushes to see Jesus (21:7).

Second, the resurrection appearance includes a meal (as it does in Luke 24). Again there is at least the strong hint that the risen Lord is made known to the community of believers in the celebration of a meal. (It may be that John's community included fish as part of the eucharistic celebration (see also John 6:1-12).)

Finally, the story includes a call to discipleship and a granting of authority (or responsibility) to Peter. This is the closest the Gospel comes to recognizing a special place in the church for Peter. Here his task of feeding the sheep may represent the responsibility of all the early church leaders.

John's Gospel therefore contains two different resurrection traditions. In John 20 the tomb and appearance traditions are conflated and set in Jerusalem. Jesus' resurrection affirms the importance of his crucifixion, and Jesus explains to Mary and the disciples the importance of his return to the Father. In John 21 we have the account of an appearance set in Galilee. In both cases we see the tenuous relationship between Peter and the beloved disciple as resurrection witnesses. In both cases the risen Lord grants authority and responsibility to the church.

Preaching on the resurrection in John

1. When preaching from John, it is impossible to preach on the resurrection without at the same time referring to the crucifixion. It is the crucifixion which is Jesus' great victory, and the resurrection confirms that victory (see John 20:17).

2. The command to Mary Magdalene, "Do not hold me," is probably a reminder to believers that our faith must be based, not alone on reminiscences of the earthly Jesus, but on an abiding relationship to the risen Lord as mediated by the Holy Spirit (John 20:17).

3. Again the risen Lord establishes the church, and its authority is derived explicitly from his gift (John 20:22-23).

4. The story of Thomas is rich with implications for an understanding of the relationship of doubt and faith in John's Gospel. Jesus does not condemn or deny Thomas' request for evidence, for a sign. Indeed, Thomas makes the statement of faith in the Gospel: "My Lord and my God!" (20:28). However, the greater blessing is reserved for those who are able to believe without such tangible signs. This is a paradigm of the relationship of seeing to believing in all of John's Gospel. There *are* signs, things to be seen which can evoke or strengthen faith. But faith is not finally faith in those signs. It is faith in the Son and in the Father who sent him. Therefore those who believe directly in the Son without needing signs are the most blessed of all (see John 20:24-29).

5. John 21 again shows the risen Lord as the one who calls people to discipleship and establishes a community, the church. Here, however, it is not so much authority which he bestows upon Peter (and the church) as it is responsibility. Their ministry is to be a ministry of service (as Jesus' ministry has been).

6. The implications of Jesus' resurrection are also spelled out in John 14, 16, and especially in John 11—the story of Lazarus. For John, Jesus is the resurrection and the life for all believers (11:25). This statement means that because of him physical death has no lasting power. It also means that the quality of this present life is "eternal." This "eternal" life is not threatened or destroyed by all the various forms of death-in-life. Of all the Gospel writers, John

makes most clear that Jesus' resurrection provides both hope for the future and redemption for the present.

What Happened Anyway? The Events Behind the Gospels

It is a truism that we have no accounts of the resurrection *per se*, but only of the events which followed the resurrection. This hardly seems crucial. For one thing it is hard to know what an account of the resurrection *per se* would look like: Reports of Jesus coming out of the tomb? Evidence of renewed activity in his brain? For another thing we *do* know what evidence led the first Christians to believe in his resurrection; and if that was enough for them, it will have to do for us as well.

We can reconstruct the development of the tradition in the following way.

Originally there were two separate traditions concerning the resurrection. Or, at least, the tradition included accounts of two separate series of events.

The empty tomb tradition centered in Jerusalem, and the women were cited as the first witnesses to the empty tomb. The appearance tradition centered in Galilee (as Mark, Matthew, and John 21 still indicate). The disciples were cited as the first witnesses to the resurrection appearances. In all probability Peter was the first disciple (indeed the first person) to see the risen Lord.

It is easy enough to see why two separate series of events are recounted in the tradition. As Mark 14:27 (and parallels in Matthew and Luke) and John 16:32 indicate, at the time of Jesus' arrest and crucifixion, most if not all of the disciples made a speedy getaway to Galilee. After all, if their leader faced execution for his activities, Jerusalem was hardly safe for them. The women, whether because they were more faithful or because they were more secure (not even Pilate was apt to crucify women), stayed in Jerusalem to perform whatever final duties seemed appropriate. Therefore the women were the ones who found the empty tomb. The disciples, who had fled to Galilee, were the first to see the risen Lord. Peter, who had denied Jesus most cruelly, was nevertheless the first to whom he appeared.

Probably as early as the confession behind 1 Corinthians 15:3-7, the two traditions had been brought together. Certainly the Gospels all bear evidence of both the empty tomb and the appearance traditions.

With the exception of Mark, the Gospel writers try to clean up the evidence that the venerated disciples had headed for the hills at the time of Jesus' arrest. Matthew suggests that the disciples went to Galilee at the explicit instruction of the risen Lord (Matthew 28:10). Luke and John (20) have the resurrection appearances to the disciples take place in Jerusalem (though Luke, as we have seen, had theological reasons, also, for placing the appearances in Jerusalem).

Luke and John have the disciples as well as the women witness the empty tomb, and Matthew and John have the risen Lord appear to women as well as to the disciples. In these ways the traditions come closer and closer together.

We can therefore say this about the early traditions regarding the resurrection events.

1. All the witnesses bear testimony to the fact that something happened. It was in response to an event (and not out of a vacuum) that the Easter faith arose. That event was somehow tied to the third day after the crucifixion.

2. Perhaps from the earliest witness (the pre-Pauline tradition) and certainly from Mark's Gospel on, two kinds of evidence were cited for the reality of the event: the evidence of the post-resurrection appearances and the evidence of the empty tomb. The appeal to the empty tomb does not seem to be a late invention of the church, and the evidence is quite good that the tomb *was* empty.

3. The accounts of the appearances differ so from one another that it is impossible to draw any firm conclusions about the nature of those appearances. They do tend to suggest that while it was Jesus who appeared, it was not the same old Jesus. In Paul's terms it was a "spiritual body." At any rate, he was not immediately recognizable as empirically precisely the same flesh, blood, and bones the disciples had known prior to the crucifixion.

Beyond that we can do nothing but hedge. We simply do not have evidence to make historical claims which are any bolder than those which I have made. The narratives do, however, draw two conclusions which are inescapable.

First, they insist on the facticity of the resurrection. There was a real (even a datable) event, and it was out of that event that the resurrection faith was born.

Second, the narratives insist on the identification of the risen Lord with the crucified Jesus. The resurrection is, if you will, an event in the history of Jesus and not just an event in the lives of believers or in the history of the church. For the New Testament, it is not the significance of Jesus or the message of Jesus or the truth of Jesus or the community around Jesus which goes marching on. It is Jesus. We may not be able to believe that, but if we believe less than that, we believe less than the unanimous witness of the New Testament.

From the belief in the reality of the resurrection events and in the identification of the risen Lord with the crucified Christ, the New Testament derived a number of implications for its faith. Those implications are the subject of our final chapter.

CHAPTER 6

The Significance of the Resurrection for Christian Faith

In the New Testament the belief in Jesus' resurrection has far-reaching implications for faith. Presumably the belief in his resurrection also has important implications for the church's faith today.

We shall consider the relationship of the belief in Jesus' resurrection to five areas of the church's faith and life.

Resurrection and Faith in Jesus' Lordship

Whatever may be the case for us, it seems clear that the early church did not come to a full faith in Jesus as Lord until after it came to believe in his resurrection. Romans 1:4 is an explicit indication of what is implicit throughout the New Testament: "[Jesus was] designated Son of God in power according to the Spirit of holiness by his resurrection from the dead." The Emmaus story suggests that the disciples did not understand the meaning of Jesus' ministry and crucifixion and especially its relationship to the Old Testament until after his resurrection (Luke 24:25-27).

Of course faith in Jesus' lordship was never compelled by the resurrection events. In Matthew 28:17, even when the disciples see the risen Jesus, some continue to doubt. Those who do perceive that Christ is risen, however, also perceive that he is Lord. They worship him (28:17).

Therefore whatever happened was not in itself enough to compel faith in Jesus' lordship. A certain receptivity, a tendency toward faith was apparently required. But the "whatever happened" was necessary, if not sufficient, to the awakening of faith. If we cannot accept the early church's version of what happened (the tomb was empty and Jesus appeared to some people), then we shall have to try to find for our time those events which can confirm Jesus' special status as God's man among us.

Perhaps (as some theologians think) Jesus' ministry and message and crucifixion can suffice to awaken our faith in his lordship. If so, we shall have to admit that we are in a better position than the earliest disciples, who apparently required something else. The something else which they required need not be tied to any particular version of what happened on the third day. However, I am inclined to think that they were right in believing that it is impossible to say both "Jesus is Lord" and "Jesus is dead" without being caught in an impossible contradiction. And the claim "Jesus *was* Lord" makes no sense at all. Jesus' lordship is not just a matter of his past achievements, but a matter of his present authority for us and of his claim on our obedience as the *living* Lord.

Resurrection and the Community of Faith

Only in Luke–Acts is the church constituted by an event which is separate from Jesus' resurrection. Elsewhere the New Testament accounts of the establishment of the church are resurrection accounts.

Several witnesses testify that the *risen* Lord founded the church. In Matthew 28:18 and following, he gives the disciples the Great Commission, which is the beginning of their ministry. In John 20:21-23 he gives the disciples the gifts of peace and the Holy Spirit and bestows on them the authority to forgive and retain sins. In John 21:15 and following, the risen Lord commissions Peter as caretaker of the church. For Paul, his own apostleship and therefore his whole view of the church's authority and mission is tied to his vision of the risen Lord (First Corinthians 15:8-10; 9:1-2), and according to our analysis, Mark 1:16-20, which is a church-founding story for Mark, is also the story of an appearance by the risen Lord.

Today, it is hard to see what sense we can make of the life of the church apart from Jesus' resurrection. The church as the body of Christ is still not just the body which remembers him, but the body which is enlivened by his life. (See Romans 12:3-7; 1 Corinthians 12:12-31; Colossians 1:18; and Ephesians 4:15-16; 5:23.)

Nor can we make sense of the ordinances, or sacraments, apart from Jesus' resurrection. Only on the odd view that the Lord's Supper is a memorial service for a departed friend can we possibly celebrate communion apart from the faith in the real presence of the Lord as host at his table. The faith in his presence requires the faith that he is alive and, therefore, the faith that he is risen. It is this faith which the Emmaus story of Luke 24:13-35 affirms. Baptism for Paul and for most Christians since Paul is still a participation in Christ's death and resurrection, as the new Christian, however symbolically, dies to sin and rises to a new life of faithfulness (see Romans 6:1-11). Therefore, if Christ is not risen, baptism is a sham.

Preaching, unless Christ is risen, is a dull report of distant historical facts or urgent moral exhortation. If Christ is risen and present in the preached word, then preaching can be a channel of new life. What the preacher presents is no longer a word about an historical figure, but the living Word himself. It is Christ himself who challenges and comforts the hearer. If Christ is not risen and present in the preached word, then the preacher had best be still.

Further, the whole idea of the communion of saints is not the idea of communion simply with one another. The fellowship of the church is seen from the beginning as fellowship in Christ. The metaphors shift. Sometimes we are his sheep, sometimes his body, sometimes the branches of the true vine. The reality is remarkably constant. The church is herself only because she is his, not only in memory, but in faith and hope. The communion of saints includes the saints who have died, because they are also his. Like us they are sustained by the love and mercy of the risen Lord.

Finally, the risen Lord not only enlivens the church, he also judges the church. He is Lord not only of the believers but of the whole creation (as, for instance, 1 Corinthians 15:24 makes clear). Matthew's Gospel especially affirms that the risen Christ is present not only in the church but over against the church. He stands in judgment against her hypocrisies and calls her to account, demanding that she minister to the least of his brothers (Matthew 25, especially verses 31-46).

Resurrection and Life After Death

It needs to be said that the problem of life after death is only a minor theme in Mark, Matthew, and Luke. These Gospels affirm the belief in the resurrection of the dead without explicitly deriving that belief from Jesus' resurrection. (See Mark 12:18-27; Matthew 22:23-33; Luke 20:27-40.) Matthew does indicate a preliminary resurrection of the saints at the time of Jesus' crucifixion and resurrection, however (Matthew 27:52-53). And we have suggested that Mark's stories of Jairus' daughter and of the boy seized by a demon are used by Mark to indicate the life-giving power of the risen Lord.

Indeed in New Testament theology in general, the resurrection of Jesus is seen first of all to be an event which has implications for Jesus' role and significance, second as an event which has implications for the course of human history, and only third as an event which has implications for the life of the individual after death.

However, for Paul and John, Jesus' resurrection does have implications for the death and resurrection of others. Paul sees Jesus' resurrection as the first instance of the general resurrection. Furthermore, Jesus' resurrection has life-giving power for all. Because of Jesus' resurrection, we can be sure that the general resurrection has begun. At the end, all people shall rise as "spiritual bodies." That is, they shall rise as themselves but not as the *same* selves (1 Corinthians 15:20-23, 35-50).

In John's Gospel "eternal life" refers first to the quality of earthly life, but there is also a future element to that life. Jesus' claim to be the resurrection and the life has implications for the believer both in the present and after death: "He who believes in me, though he die, yet shall he live, and whoever lives and believes in me shall never die" (John 11:25-26). Paul's belief in a general resurrection at the end of time has been partly altered. John apparently believes that the individual enters into the eternal life-after-death at the time of death: "When I go and prepare a place for you, I will come again and will take you to myself, that where I am you may be also." (John 14:3. John 5:25-29, however, preserves the idea of a general resurrection, and even the saying in John 14:3 *could* point to a general resurrection.)

Paul and John suggest that Jesus' resurrection has these implications for our own view of death.

First, Jesus' resurrection makes clear that death does not overcome God. For the faithful person, the primary reality is not oneself but God. The primary comfort is that death—whatever other terrors it may entail—does not entail the death of God. Jesus' resurrection proclaims that God lives, despite all the evidence to the contrary. Jesus' resurrection proclaims that death, whatever else it negates, does not negate the power of God.

Second, the resurrection makes clear that death does not negate the individual person. Paul's labored attempt to explain the notion of a "spiritual body" can serve as a warning that we will have to do without descriptions of the risen individual or of the kingdom of heaven. However, the resurrection faith does affirm that the individual is not overcome by death. Most modestly, this means that the individual is still loved and accepted by God despite death, that "whether we live or whether we die, we are the Lord's" (Romans 14:8).

Third, less modestly, Paul, at least, sees Jesus as representative of all humankind and his resurrection as representative of our resurrection (1 Corinthians 15:21-22). If we are to assume, with the New Testament, that what God raised was not Jesus' memory or his message but his person, then on Paul's terms we must assume that God will raise us as persons, too. Beyond that affirmation (vague as it is) there is room only for poetry or faith or both. And there is also room for the reminder that the value of eternal life is not that it is life which goes on and on, but that it is life in God.

Resurrection and the Goal of History

As Paul especially makes clear, Jesus' resurrection is a sign and promise for the future, not just for individuals, but for the whole of human history. (See Romans 8:34; 1 Corinthians 15:20-28. The whole of the section which follows is really an interpretation of Romans 8 and 1 Corinthians 15.) That is, Jesus' resurrection provides a clue for the understanding of eschatology. For Paul, at least, Jesus' resurrection is the first event of the last days, and the doctrine of last days must be interpreted in the light of Jesus' resurrection. This premise has the following implications.

First, Jesus' resurrection indicates that history has a *telos*, a goal toward which it moves. Just when Jesus' history seemed to have ended in devastating futility, the resurrection affirmed that his history moved purposefully toward a redemptive goal. The resurrection becomes the sign of the fact that God moves *all* of history toward his redeeming purpose. In Jesus' resurrection the very course of history was reversed, and the new age of fulfillment began.

History's goal can be seen in temporal terms, as if it were the last scene in the drama. It can be seen in metaphysical terms, as if it were the intent of the Author whether the drama has a proper ending or not. This means that history moves from a purpose (which is called creation) toward a purpose (which is called the eschaton). There are as many ways of explaining that metaphysically as there are metaphysics. At least the resurrection rules out any understanding of human history which appeals to futility.

Second, Jesus' resurrection indicates that the right meaning of history's goal is to be seen in the life and death of Jesus of Nazareth. Of course we only see through a glass darkly, but the glass is the glass whose design is Jesus Christ. What that means is worth books, not sentences. It means, at the least, that suffering is not an accidental fluke in an otherwise sensible history, but is rather part of its sense. It means that faithful defeat counts for more than apostate victory. It means that love is an easy word and a hard reality, but the hard reality is worth more than all the cheap words.

Third, Jesus' resurrection reminds us that history has surprises. Here R. R. Niebuhr is certainly right in seeing that the fundamental categories we must choose between are resurrection and law.[1] According to law it is all over for us, from the first Freudian goof on the part of our parents or from the genetic programming of our remotest ancestors. According to resurrection, history has room for a few novelties. Because history has room for surprises, the course of history, like the course of our lives, can be surprisingly and graciously changed.

Fourth, Jesus' resurrection reminds us that judgment is a reality which transcends personal guilt or self-satisfaction and which also transcends community mores or regulations. In John 21 Jesus' confrontation with the Peter who has denied him symbolizes the judgment and the mercy which outlast even death. As Matthew 25 reminds us, final judgment means that what we do in the secret places of our hearts counts. As the whole New Testament reminds us, final mercy means that what Jesus did on the cross also counts, even more.

Fifth, Jesus' resurrection shows that God not only *will* act, he already is acting. Jesus' resurrection indicates that the signs of God's kingdom appear today and not only tomorrow. Jesus' resurrection indicates that God's kingdom keeps constant pressure on the kingdoms of this world. It indicates not just that the kingdom is yet to come, but that the kingdom *is* coming.

Finally, the resurrection as a clue to the goal of history indicates that the destiny of each of us is bound up with the destiny of all of us. Indeed, the destiny of each of us is bound up with the destiny of the whole created universe. Jesus' resurrection is an event which not only vindicates *his* life, but which promises vindication for the whole creation. "The creation waits with eager longing for the revealing of the sons of God" (Romans 8:19).

There is one final problem which Jesus' resurrection poses for our understanding of history's goal. We are inclined to think that any adequate interpretation of eschatology would avoid temporal language. Stories about Jesus returning on a particular day with given sound effects strike us as mythological if not ludicrous. Yet the matter is not as simple as that. For religions whose concern is with eternal truths, the translation of eschatology into nontemporal categories might make some sense. For a faith which is un-ashamedly if not unconfusedly historical, such a translation does not work nearly as well. For the Christian, time is not an embarrassment to the transcendent God. It is the stage on which he operates. If atonement happened on Friday and eternal life on Sunday (which in part they did, given Christian categories), then we cannot simply say that it is nonsensical to talk of times and seasons for consummation. We do not know when it is going to happen, but perhaps there has to be a *whenness* for it to count as happening at all.

The Life of the Believer in the Light of the Resurrection

Life in the light of Jesus' resurrection is life under Jesus' lordship. Because it is life under Jesus' lordship, it is marked by the fullness of faith and hope and love which he offers to those who follow him. It therefore has as many different shapes as the lives of those who aspire to faith, hope, and love.

Life in the light of Jesus' resurrection is life which accepts and expects the genuinely new. It is life which is not bound to old fears, old guilt, old mistakes, or even old dogmas. It is life which is willing and eager to be surprised and therefore willing and eager to be forgiven.

Life in the light of Jesus' resurrection is life which can live in communion with the living Christ. For some, that kind of language, like the reality to which it points, has more meaning than for others. Certainly the traditional concepts of praying to Jesus or of praying to the Father through the Son depend on a faith in the risen Lord. Other more directly mystical forms of Christian devotion also derive from the belief that Christ is risen.

Life in the light of Jesus' resurrection is life which is not bound by the reality of death. Death need not be only physical death, threatening as that is. There is a kind of death, a kind of negation of ourselves in despair, when we cannot accept our own selfhood. There is a kind of death in hatred, when we are controlled by another rather than being able to define our own relationship to that other. There is a kind of death in all those fears which destroy our ability to choose and to care. Jesus' resurrection is God's No to the finality and authority of any of these deaths. Any victory over such deaths is a resurrection. According to the Christian faith, any victory over such deaths is Christ's victory.

Life in the light of the resurrection is also life in community. Because resurrection is the victory over fear, it is also the victory over self-absorption. That victory alone can make community possible. Life in the light of the resurrection is also life in community because it is life in Christ. In Christ there is no room for isolation or self-absorption. Right Christian confession always refers to Jesus Christ as *our* Lord.

The resurrection of Jesus of Nazareth is therefore at the very heart of the church's faith. The church understands Jesus' lordship, her own life, the threat of death, the goal of history, and the possibilities of human existence all in the light of his resurrection.

Conclusion:
Fact and Faith
in Interpreting
the New Testament

Our understanding of miracles and resurrection in the New Testament provides some essential clues to our understanding of the richness of the New Testament faith.

Miracles and resurrection provide a clue to the New Testament understanding of the nature of God. In the stories of miracles and of Jesus' resurrection, the New Testament affirms its faith both in God's immanence and in God's transcendence. The God who works miracles and who raised Jesus from the dead is a God who really does things in human history. Events which are experienced by ordinary people (however extraordinary the events) are the signs of God's involvement in human lives and in human history. He is involved in matters as mundane as a blind man who wants to see, a paralytic lowered through a roof, an empty tomb, an ecstatic experience on the Damascus Road. But God also transcends all of those historical events. A description of what happened is never a sufficient indication of the transcendent power of God. The New Testament moves from descriptions of blind men healed to affirmations about God's judgment (John 9). It moves from descriptions of a paralytic walking to the claim that God in Jesus Christ forgives sins. It moves from the empty tomb and the

Damascus Road to the astonishing claim that God is sovereign in all of human history and will redeem the whole creation by his grace. The mundane events are central to the New Testament understanding of who God is, but they do not begin to exhaust that understanding. The New Testament constantly moves from the empirical facts to the astonishing claims of faith. God acts in human history, but he is also beyond human history. God reveals himself to our understanding, but he is also beyond both our understanding and our imagining.

Miracles and resurrection also provide a clue to the New Testament understanding of the relationship of grace and faith. Miracles and resurrection provide a meeting place for God's grace and our faith. The events themselves are God's gracious recognition of our humanity. Most of us, at least, cannot really comprehend him in the abstract. We do need signs, tangible, visible clues to his presence and his purpose. We cannot reason our way to him or pray our way to him unless he has first found the ways to show himself to us. The events themselves, miracles and resurrection, are sheer grace.

But it takes faith to respond to those events and to see them as miracles. It takes faith to perceive that they are not just unusual events. The same miracles which the faithful ascribe to God, the unfaithful can ascribe to Satan. The empty tomb can evoke faith in the God who raises people from the dead or it can evoke the suspicion that someone stole the body. Even the resurrection appearance to the disciples could not prevent some from doubting. The events in themselves can always be described more prosaically than as the acts of a merciful God. It takes faith to recognize them as his works.

The relationship between grace and faith is yet more complex than that. Sometimes, at least, faith itself is seen as a gift. It is God who does the miracle and God who provides the faith to see the miracle. That is why the father of the boy who is possessed can pray: "I believe; help my unbelief!" (Mark 9:24).

Finally, our understanding of miracles and resurrection provides clues for understanding the New Testament's affirmations about God's incarnation in Jesus of Nazareth. The whole incarnation is a kind of miracle. As with the other miracles, God's activity in Jesus was visible, tangible. In Jesus, God entered into the everyday empirical world and made himself known in concrete historical events. However, the concrete historical events were not enough to compel the recognition that God was active in this man Jesus. The events, the acts, and the words themselves led some to believe only that he was a wandering magician and preacher or, worse than that, a troublemaker who threatened the laws of God and the state. It took faith to perceive in those odd events the signs of God's activity. It took faith to perceive in that odd man the fullness of God's loving revelation of himself. As with the New Testament understanding of miracles and resurrection, the New Testament understanding of Jesus requires both a respect for what has happened in history, and a faith which can perceive what has happened in history as the activity of God himself.

God's incarnation in Jesus Christ is the central miracle of the New Testament. Therefore, the other miracles, and even the miracle of the resurrection, are not held to be important in themselves. They are important because they point to Jesus. They bear witness to the fact that God is active in Jesus. They indicate the ways in which God is active in Jesus—judging, forgiving, loving, and redeeming humankind.

The stories of miracles and of the resurrection were used from the beginning as we should use them today. They were used to point to Jesus as the incarnation of the living God. They were used as signs of the ways in which God was active in Jesus Christ. They were used to evoke faith in Jesus Christ, not just as a miracle worker, but as the gift and revealer of God's own love.

Footnotes

Chapter 1

[1] Ernst and Marie-Luise Keller, *Miracles in Dispute: A Continuing Debate* (London: SCM Press Ltd., 1969), p. 70.

[2] See Rudolf Bultmann, *The History of the Synoptic Tradition*, trans. John Marsh (New York: Harper & Row, Publishers, 1963), p. 162.

[3] *Ibid.*, p. 35.

[4] Formally, the "normal" exorcism story can be analyzed in five parts: (1) meeting of the exorcist with the demoniac; (2) the warding-off cry of the demons; (3) Jesus' effective exorcistic command; (4) the success of the exorcism; and (5) the amazement of the onlookers. The inordinately curious can find evidence for this formal analysis in my Ph.D. dissertation, *Exorcism Stories in the Gospel of Mark* (Yale University, 1972), pp. 36-58.

Chapter 2

[1] For a lengthy analysis, see Austin Farrer, *St. Matthew and St. Mark* (London: Dacre Press, 1954), pp. 57-80.

[2] Paul J. Achtemeier, "Toward the Isolation of Pre-Markan Miracle Catenae" in *Journal of Biblical Literature*, vol. 89, no. 2 (September, 1970), pp. 265-291; D. L. Bartlett, *Exorcism Stories in the Gospel of Mark*. Unpublished dissertation (Yale University, 1972), pp. 226-229.

[3] That "little effort" can be found in D. L. Bartlett, *op. cit.*, pp. 38-46.

[4] See Werner H. Kelber, *The Kingdom in Mark* (Philadelphia: Fortress Press, 1974), p. 15.

[5] This is argued at length in my dissertation, D. L. Bartlett, *op. cit.*, pp. 138-158.

[6] *Ibid.*, pp. 229-239.

[7] See G. H. Boobyer, "Galilee and Galileans in St. Mark's Gospel" in *The Bulletin of the John Rylands Library*, vol. 35, no. 2 (March, 1953), pp. 334 ff.; and G. Schille, *Anfänge der Kirche* (Munich, 1966), pp. 175-178.

[8] Walter Bauer, *A Greek-English Lexicon of the New Testament and Other Early Christian Literature*, trans. W. F. Arndt and F. W. Gingrich (Chicago: University of Chicago Press, 1957), 4th ed., p. 659.

[9] See Austin Farrer, *op. cit.*, p. 91.

[10] B. W. Bacon stressed the division into five sections, though unlike me he thought that each sermon was most closely linked with the *preceding* narrative material. See B. W. Bacon, *Studies in Matthew* (New York: Holt, Rinehart and Winston, Inc., 1930).

[11] See Günther Bornkamm, Gerhard Barth, and Heinz Joachim Held, *Tradition and Interpretation in Matthew*, trans. P. Scott (Philadelphia: The Westminster

Press, 1963), pp. 165-299.

[12] On this passage see Reginald H. Fuller, *Interpreting the Miracles* (London: SCM Press Ltd., 1963), p. 78.

[13] Considerable amounts of this analysis are based on Hans Conzelmann, *The Theology of St. Luke,* trans. Geoffrey Buswell (London: Farber & Farber, 1961).

[14] A number of insights in this section were suggested by R. H. Fuller, *op. cit.,* pp. 82-87.

[15] Rudolf Bultmann, *Theology of the New Testament,* vol. 2, trans. Kendrick Grobel (New York: Charles Scribner's Sons, 1955), p. 40; Ernst Käsemann, *The Testament of Jesus* (Philadelphia: Fortress Press, 1968), p. 6.

[16] Some of the following analysis is based on Raymond E. Brown, ed. and trans., *The Anchor Bible: The Gospel According to John,* vol. 29 (New York: Doubleday & Company, Inc., 1966), pp. 525-532.

Chapter 3

[1] Cited in Hermann Strack and Paul Billerbeck, *Kommentar zum Neuen Testament aus Talmud und Midrasch,* vol. 4 (Munich: C. H. Beck'sche Verlagbuchhandlung, 1928), p. 507.

[2] *Ibid.,* p. 507.

[3] For texts and discussion, see my dissertation, Bartlett, *Exorcism Stories in the Gospel of Mark* (Yale University, 1972), pp. 94 ff.

[4] Lucian, *The Loeb Classical Library Edition,* trans. A. M. Harmon (Cambridge: Harvard University Press, 1960), p. 345.

[5] "Testament of Simeon," 6:5-6, *Apocrypha and Pseudepigrapha of the Old Testament,* vol. 2 (Oxford: The Clarendon Press, 1963), p. 303.

[6] Paul Tillich, *Systematic Theology,* vol. 3 (Chicago: The University of Chicago Press, 1963), p. 103.

[7] I am not sure how far the phenomenon evident in this analysis corresponds to "resistance" in the process of psychotherapy. For a discussion of the term, see James E. Dittes, *The Church in the Way* (New York: Charles Scribner's Sons, 1967), pp. 45-86.

[8] An example of a psychoanalytical attempt to "explain" a case of "possession" (in this case a pact with the devil) is found in Sigmund Freud, "A Neurosis of Demonical Possession in the Seventeenth Century," in *Studies of Parapsychology* (New York: The Macmillan Company, 1963), pp. 91 ff.

Chapter 4

[1] See Hugh J. Schonfield, *The Passover Plot* (New York: Bernard Geis Associates, 1965).

[2] Richard R. Niebuhr, *Resurrection and Historical Reason: A Study of Theological Method* (New York: Charles Scribner's Sons, 1957), p. 155.

Chapter 5

[1] See Reginald H. Fuller, *The Formation of the Resurrection Narratives* (New York: The Macmillan Company, 1971), p. 29.

[2] See Willi Marxsen, *The Resurrection of Jesus of Nazareth,* trans. Margaret Kohl (Philadelphia: Fortress Press, 1970), p. 80; Fuller, *op. cit.,* p. 52.

[3] *Ibid.,* p. 16. Fuller points out that the reference to burial in 1 Corinthians 15:4*a* occurs within a separate *hoti* ("that") clause and therefore is clearly separated by tradition from the preceding reference to death and the succeeding reference to appearances.

[4] *Ibid.,* p. 16.

[5]*Ibid.*, p. 23; for another attempt at explanation, see C. F. Evans, *Resurrection and the New Testament* (Naperville, Ill.: Alec. R. Allenson, Inc., 1970), pp. 48ff.

[6]Willi Marxsen argues that Peter was the first to come to the resurrection faith—he did not actually *see* anyone—and that the faith of the other "witnesses" derived from Peter's. However, the same verb "appeared" is used for the whole set of witnesses, and there seems to be no reason to single Peter out, apart from the fact that he was the first to whom Jesus appeared. See Marxsen, *op. cit.*, pp. 125, 95-96.

[7]Evans, *op. cit.*, p. 55.

[8]Marxsen, *op. cit.*

[9]Although he does not translate the text as I do, Günther Bornkamm also holds that this passage gives no account of the *content* of the experience on the Damascus Road. G. Bornkamm, *Paul*, trans. D. M. G. Stalker (London: Hodder & Stoughton, 1971), p. 17.

[10]See, for example, the articles of P. Vielhauer and E. R. Goodenough in Leander E. Keck and J. Louis Martyn, eds., *Studies in Luke-Acts* (Nashville: Abingdon Press, 1966), pp. 33-59.

[11]Fuller, *op. cit.*, p. 46.

[12]*Ibid.*, p. 20.

[13]See further Evans, *op. cit.*, pp. 67-68, for the possibilities and their attendant problems.

[14]Robert H. Lightfoot, *The Gospel Message of St. Mark* (Oxford: The Clarendon Press, 1950), pp. 80-98; Ernst Lohmeyer, *Das Evangelium des Markus* (Göttingen: Vandenhoech & Ruprecht, 1951), pp. 356-360; Willi Marxsen, *Mark the Evangelist*, trans. R. A. Harrisville (Nashville: Abingdon Press, 1969), pp. 75-92.

[15]See Marxsen, *Mark the Evangelist;* Weeden; Perrin; Lohmeyer in footnotes and bibliography.

[16]For a more complete argument on this and other points in this section, see my dissertation, Bartlett, *Exorcism Stories in the Gospel of Mark* (Yale University, 1972), pp. 229-239.

[17]See Robert H. Lightfoot, *Locality and Doctrine in the Gospels* (New York: Harper & Row, Publishers, 1937), p. 111.

[18]Evans also suggests this possibility; Evans, *op. cit.*, p. 53.

[19]Fuller thinks that Luke may also have used a special source of his own; Fuller, *op. cit.*, pp. 95 ff.

[20]See *ibid.*, pp. 96-97, for a discussion of the pair.

[21]For a full discussion, see *ibid.*, pp. 120-130.

[22]See Bruce M. Metzger, ed., *A Textual Commentary on the Greek New Testament* (London: United Bible Societies, 1971), pp. 189-190.

[23]There is a more detailed discussion of all this in Fuller, *op. cit.*, pp. 120-130.

[24]See Marxsen, *op. cit.*, p. 58 ff. Marxsen is mistaken, though, in seeing here any indication that Peter believed on the basis of the empty tomb.

Chapter 6

[1]Richard R. Niebuhr, *Resurrection and Historical Reason: A Study of Theological Method* (New York: Charles Scribner's Sons, 1957), p. 155.

Suggested Bibliography

Bacon, Benjamin Wisner, *Studies in Matthew*. New York: Holt, Rinehart and Winston, Inc., 1930.

Barrett, C. K., *The Gospel According to St. John*. New York: The Seabury Press, 1962.

Bartlett, D. L., *Exorcism Stories in the Gospel of Mark*. Unpublished dissertation, Yale University, 1972.

Bornkamm, G., Barth, G., Held, H. J., *Tradition and Interpretation in Matthew*, trans. P. Scott. Philadelphia: The Westminster Press, 1963.

Brown, Raymond E., ed. and trans., *The Anchor Bible: The Gospel According to John*, 2 vols. New York: Doubleday & Company, Inc., 1970.

Bultmann, Rudolf, *The History of the Synoptic Tradition*, trans. John Marsh. New York: Harper & Row, Publishers, 1963.

____, *Theology of the New Testament*, 2 vols., trans. Kendrick Grobel, New York: Charles Scribner's Sons, 1970.

Caird, G. B., ed., *Gospel of St. Luke*. Harmondsworth, England: Penguin Books Inc., 1963.

Conzelmann, Hans, *The Theology of St. Luke*, trans. G. Buswell. London: Faber & Faber, 1961.

Dibelius, Martin, *From Tradition to Gospel*, trans. B. L. Wolff. Greenwood, S. C.: Attic Press, 1972.

Dittes, James E., *The Church in the Way*. New York: Charles Scribner's Sons, 1967.

Evans, Christopher F., *Resurrection and the New Testament*. Naperville, Ill.: Alec. R. Allenson, Inc., 1970.

Evely, Louis, *The Gospels Without Myth*, trans. J. F. Bernard. New York: Doubleday & Company, Inc., 1971.

Fuller, Reginald H., *Interpreting the Miracles*. London: SCM Press Ltd., 1963.

——, *The Formation of the Resurrection Narratives*. New York: The Macmillan Company, 1971.

Keller, Ernst and Marie-Luise, *Miracles in Dispute: A Continuing Debate*. London: SCM Press Ltd., 1969.

Lewis, C. S., *Miracles: A Preliminary Study*. New York: The Macmillan Company, 1963.

Lightfoot, Robert H., *Locality and Doctrine in the Gospels*. New York: Harper & Row, Publishers, 1937.

Martyn, James Louis, *History and Theology in the Fourth Gospel*. New York: Harper & Row, Publishers, 1968.

Marxsen, Willi, *Mark the Evangelist*, trans. R. A. Harrisville. Nashville: Abingdon Press, 1969.

——, *The Resurrection of Jesus of Nazareth,* trans. M. Kohl. Philadelphia: Fortress Press, 1970.

Moule, Charles F. D., ed., *Miracles: Cambridge Studies in Their Philosophy and History*. Naperville, Ill.: Alec. R. Allenson, Inc., 1965.

——, ed., *The Significance of the Message of the Resurrection for Faith in Jesus Christ*. Naperville, Ill.: Alec. R. Allenson, Inc., 1968.

Niebuhr, Richard R., *Resurrection and Historical Reason*. New York: Charles Scribner's Sons, 1957.

Perrin, Norman, *Rediscovering the Teaching of Jesus*. New York: Harper & Row, Publishers, 1967.

Ramsey, Ian T., *Religious Language*. New York: The Macmillan Company, 1963.

Richardson, Alan, *The Miracle Stories of the Gospels*. Naperville, Ill.: Alec. R. Allenson, Inc., 1963.

Robinson, James M., *The Problem of History in Mark*. Naperville, Ill.: Alec. R. Allenson, Inc., 1957.

Schweizer, Eduard, *The Good News According to Mark*. Richmond: John Knox Press, 1970.

Swinburne, Richard, *The Concept of Miracle*. New York: St. Martin's Press, Inc., 1971.

Taylor, Vincent, *The Gospel According to St. Mark*. New York: St. Martin's Press, Inc., 1963.

Van Der Loos, H., *The Miracles of Jesus*. Leiden: E. J. Brill, 1965.

Weeden, Theodore J., *Mark: Traditions in Conflict*. Philadelphia: Fortress Press, 1971.

Index of New Testament